Cram101 Textbook Outlines to accompany:

International Business Law and Its Environment

Richard Schaffer, 6th Edition

A Cram101 Inc. publication (c) 2010.

PRACTICE EXAMS.

Get all of the self-teaching practice exams for each chapter of this textbook at **www.Cram101.com** and ace the tests. Here is an example:

Chapter 1

International Business Law and Its Environment
Richard Schaffer, 6th Edition,
All Material Written and Prepared by Cram101

Competition law history refers to attempts by governments to regulate competitive markets for goods and services, leading up to the modern competition or antitrust laws around the world today. The earliest records traces back to the efforts of Roman legislators to control price fluctuations and unfair trade practices. Through the Middle Ages in Europe, Kings and Queens repeatedly cracked down on monopolies, including those created through state legislation.

I WANT A BETTER GRADE.   Items 1 - 50 of 100.

1 _____ is a policy or ideology of violence intended to intimidate or cause terror for the purpose of "exerting pressure on decision making by state bodies." The term "terror" is largely used to indicate clandestine, low-intensity violence that targets civilians and generates public fear. Thus "terror" is distinct from asymmetric warfare, and violates the concept of a common law of war in which civilian life is regarded. The term "-ism" is used to indicate an ideology --typically one that claims its attacks are in the domain of a "just war" concept, though most condemn such as crimes against humanity.

　○ Terrorism   ○ Table A
　○ Tacit relocation   ○ Tag-along right

2
· Apostolic _____ (a class of Roman Catholic Church documents)
· _____ of the Roman Republic
· Constitutional court

You get a 50% discount for the online exams. Go to **Cram101.com**, click Sign Up at the top of the screen, and enter DK73DW9805 in the promo code box on the registration screen. Access to Cram101.com is $4.95 per month, cancel at any time.

With Cram101.com online, you also have access to extensive reference material.

You will nail those essays and papers. Here is an example from a Cram101 Biology text:

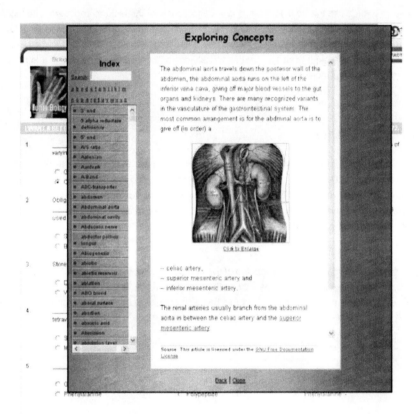

Visit **www.Cram101.com**, click Sign Up at the top of the screen, and enter DK73DW9805 in the promo code box on the registration screen. Access to www.Cram101.com is normally $9.95 per month, but because you have purchased this book, your access fee is only $4.95 per month, cancel at any time. Sign up and stop highlighting textbooks forever.

Learning System

Cram101 Textbook Outlines is a learning system. The notes in this book are the highlights of your textbook, you will never have to highlight a book again.

How to use this book. Take this book to class, it is your notebook for the lecture. The notes and highlights on the left hand side of the pages follow the outline and order of the textbook. All you have to do is follow along while your instructor presents the lecture. Circle the items emphasized in class and add other important information on the right side. With Cram101 Textbook Outlines you'll spend less time writing and more time listening. Learning becomes more efficient.

Cram101.com Online

Increase your studying efficiency by using Cram101.com's practice tests and online reference material. It is the perfect complement to Cram101 Textbook Outlines. Use self-teaching matching tests or simulate in-class testing with comprehensive multiple choice tests, or simply use Cram's true and false tests for quick review. Cram101.com even allows you to enter your in-class notes for an integrated studying format combining the textbook notes with your class notes.

Visit **www.Cram101.com**, click Sign Up at the top of the screen, and enter **DK73DW9805** in the promo code box on the registration screen. Access to www.Cram101.com is normally $9.95 per month, but because you have purchased this book, your access fee is only $4.95 per month. Sign up and stop highlighting textbooks forever.

International Business Law and Its Environment
Richard Schaffer, 6th

CONTENTS

Terrorism	Terrorism is a policy or ideology of violence intended to intimidate or cause terror for the purpose of "exerting pressure on decision making by state bodies." The term "terror" is largely used to indicate clandestine, low-intensity violence that targets civilians and generates public fear. Thus "terror" is distinct from asymmetric warfare, and violates the concept of a common law of war in which civilian life is regarded. The term "-ism" is used to indicate an ideology --typically one that claims its attacks are in the domain of a "just war" concept, though most condemn such as crimes against humanity.

Constitution

· Apostolic Constitution (a class of Roman Catholic Church documents)
· Constitution of the Roman Republic
· Constitutional court
· Constitutionalism
· Corporate Constitution
· Judicial activism
· Judicial restraint
· Judicial review

Judicial philosophies of Constitutional interpretation (note: generally specific to United States Constitutional law)

· List of national Constitutions
· Originalism
· Strict constructionism
· Textualism
· Proposed European Union Constitution

· Treaty of Lisbon (adopts same changes, but without Constitutional name)
· United Nations Charter

United States

· History of competition law
· Monopoly

· Coercive monopoly
· Natural monopoly
· Barriers to entry
· Market power
· SSNIP test
· Relevant market
· Merger control

Anti-competitive practices

· Monopolization
· Collusion

- Formation of cartels
- Price fixing
- Bid rigging
- Product bundling and tying
- Refusal to deal

  - Group boycott
  - Exclusive dealing
  - Dividing territories
  - Conscious parallelism
  - Predatory pricing
  - Misuse of patents and copyrights

Laws and doctrines

United States

- Sherman Antitrust Act
- Clayton Antitrust Act
- Robinson-Patman Act
- FTC Act
- Hart-Scott-Rodino Act
- Merger guidelines
- Essential facilities doctrine
- Noerr-Pennington doctrine
- Parker immunity doctrine
- Rule of reason

Europe

- UK competition law
- Irish competition law

Australia

  - Trade Practices Act 1974

Enforcement authorities and organizations

Competition law history refers to attempts by governments to regulate competitive markets for goods and services, leading up to the modern competition or antitrust laws around the world today. The earliest records traces back to the efforts of Roman legislators to control price fluctuations and unfair trade practices. Through the Middle Ages in Europe, Kings and Queens repeatedly cracked down on monopolies, including those created through state legislation.

  - International Competition Network
  - List of competition regulators

Business

There are many ways in which a business may be owned under the legal system of England and Wales.

Different types of ownership are suitable for organisations depending on the degree of control the owners wish to have over the business. The choice of ownership methor also relates to the organisations ability to raise funds for the business activities.

Competition law

Competition law, known in the United States as antitrust law, has three main elements:

· prohibiting agreements or practices that restrict free trading and competition between business entities. This includes in particular the repression of cartels.
· banning abusive behavior by a firm dominating a market, or anti-competitive practices that tend to lead to such a dominant position.

Pollution

Pollution is the introduction of contaminants into an environment that causes instability, disorder, harm or discomfort to the ecosystem i.e. physical systems or living organisms . Pollution can take the form of chemical substances, or energy, such as noise, heat, or light energy. Pollutants, the elements of Pollution, can be foreign substances or energies, or naturally occurring; when naturally occurring, they are considered contaminants when they exceed natural levels.

Job description

A Job description is a list of the general tasks and responsibilities of a position. Typically, it also includes to whom the position reports, specifications such as the qualifications needed by the person in the job, salary range for the position, etc. A Job description is usually developed by conducting a job analysis, which includes examining the tasks and sequences of tasks necessary to perform the job.

Waiver

A waiver is the voluntary relinquishment or surrender of some known right or privilege.
While a waiver is often in writing, sometimes a person"s actions can act as a waiver. An example of a written waiver is a disclaimer, which becomes a waiver when accepted.

Tariff

A Tariff is a duty imposed on goods when they are moved across a political boundary. They are usually associated with protectionism, the economic policy of restraining trade between nations. For political reasons, Tariff s are usually imposed on imported goods, although they may also be imposed on exported goods.

Sourcing

In business, the term word Sourcing refers to a number of procurement practices, aimed at finding, evaluating and engaging suppliers of goods and services:

· Global Sourcing a procurement strategy aimed at exploiting global efficiencies in production
· Strategic Sourcing a component of supply chain management, for improving and re-evaluating purchasing activities
- · Co Sourcing a type of auditing service
· Low-cost country Sourcing a procurement strategy for acquiring materials from countries with lower labour and production costs in order to cut operating expenses
· Corporate Sourcing a supply chain, purchasing/procurement, and inventory function
· Second-tier Sourcing a practice of rewarding suppliers for attempting to achieve minority-owned business spending goals of their customer
· Net Sourcing , a practice of utilizing an established group of businesses, individuals, or hardware ' software applications to streamline or initiate procurement practices by tapping in to and working through a third party provider
· Inverted Sourcing a price volatility reduction strategy usually conducted by procurement or supply-chain person by which the value of an organization"s waste-stream is maximized by actively seeking out the highest price possible from a range of potential buyers exploiting price trends and other market factors
· Multi Sourcing , a strategy that treats a given function, such as IT, as a portfolio of activities, some of which should be outsourced and others of which should be performed by internal staff.
· Crowd Sourcing , using an undefined, generally large group of people or community in the form of an open call to perform a task
In journalism, it can also refer to:

· Journalism Sourcing the practice of identifying a person or publication that gives information
· Single Sourcing the reuse of content in publishing
In computing, it can refer to:

· Open Sourcing the act of releasing previously proprietary software under an open source/free software license
· Power Sourcing equipment, network devices that will provide power in a Power over Ethernet (PoE) setup .

Patent

A patent is a set of exclusive rights granted by a state to an inventor or his assignee for a limited period of time in exchange for a disclosure of an invention.

The procedure for granting patent s, the requirements placed on the patent ee and the extent of the exclusive rights vary widely between countries according to national laws and international agreements. Typically, however, a patent application must include one or more claims defining the invention which must be new, inventive, and useful or industrially applicable.

Trademark

A trademark or trade mark is a distinctive sign or indicator used by an individual, business organization and to distinguish its products or services from those of other entities.
A trademark is designated by the following symbols:

· â„¢ (for an unregistered trademark that is, a mark used to promote or brand goods);
· â„ (for an unregistered service mark, that is, a mark used to promote or brand services); and
· Â® (for a registered trademark)

A trademark is a type of intellectual property, and typically a name, word, phrase, logo, symbol, design, image, or a combination of these elements. There is also a range of non-conventional trademark s comprising marks which do not fall into these standard categories.

The owner of a registered trademark may commence legal proceedings for trademark infringement to prevent unauthorized use of that trademark

Numerary	Numerary is a civil designation for persons who are incorporated in a fixed or permanent way to a society or group: regular member of the working staff, permanent staff distinguished from a super Numerary . The term Numerary and its counterpart, "super Numerary ," originated in Spanish and Latin American academy and government; it is now also used in countries all over the world, such as France, the U.S., England, Italy, etc. There are Numerary members of surgical organizations, of universities, of gastronomical associations, etc.
Arbitration	Arbitration, a form of alternative dispute resolution (ADR), is a legal technique for the resolution of disputes outside the courts, wherein the parties to a dispute refer it to one or more persons (the "arbitrators", "arbiters" or "arbitral tribunal"), by whose decision (the "award") they agree to be bound. It is a settlement technique in which a third party reviews the case and imposes a decision that is legally binding for both sides. Other forms of ADR include mediation (a form of settlement negotiation facilitated by a neutral third party) and non-binding resolution by experts.
Franchising	Franchising refers to the methods of practicing and using another person"s business philosophy. The franchisor grants the independent operator the right to distribute its products, techniques, and trademarks for a percentage of gross monthly sales and a royalty fee. Various tangibles and intangibles such as national or international advertising, training, and other support services are commonly made available by the franchisor.
Federal Trade Commission	The Federal Trade Commission is an independent agency of the United States government, established in 1914 by the Federal Trade Commission Act. Its principal mission is the promotion of "consumer protection" and the elimination and prevention of what regulators perceive to be harmfully "anti-competitive" business practices, such as coercive monopoly. The Federal Trade Commission Act was one of President Wilson"s major acts against trusts.
United Nations Conference on Trade and Development	The United Nations Conference on Trade and Development was established in 1964 as a permanent intergovernmental body. It is the principal organ of the United Nations General Assembly dealing with trade, investment and development issues.

The organization"s goals are to "maximize the trade, investment and development opportunities of developing countries and assist them in their efforts to integrate into the world economy on an equitable basis." (from official website.)

Joint venture	A Joint venture is an entity formed between two or more parties to undertake economic activity together. The parties agree to create a new entity by both contributing equity, and they then share in the revenues, expenses, and control of the enterprise. The venture can be for one specific project only, or a continuing business relationship such as the Fuji Xerox Joint venture.
Mergers and acquisitions	The phrase Mergers and acquisitions refers to the aspect of corporate strategy, corporate finance and management dealing with the buying, selling and combining of different companies that can aid, finance, or help a growing company in a given industry grow rapidly without having to create another business entity. An acquisition, also known as a takeover or a buyout, is the buying of one company (the "target") by another. An acquisition may be friendly or hostile.
Participation	Participation, in addition to its dictionary definition, has specific meanings in certain areas. · Participation, the process of involving young people in projects, policy reviews or ideas to encourage decision-making and empowerment, ownership of opinion and influence in youth services and issues that affect them and promote inclusion (particularly used amongst marginalized groups I.e. homeless, BME communities or Ex-offenders) · Participation (decision making), a notion in theory of management, economics and politics · Participation (VR), a notion from virtual reality · Participation (ownership), sharing something in common with others · Participation (Finance), getting some benefit from the performance of a certain underlying asset · Participation constraint (ER modelling), a special case of a multiplicity constraint · e-Participation, refers to Participation in e-government, and is related to the involvement of the citizen in the democratic process. Participant redirects here. · Participant Productions .
Subsidiary	A subsidiary, in business matters, is an entity that is controlled by a bigger and more powerful entity. The controlled entity is called a company, corporation, or limited liability company and in some cases can be a government or state-owned enterprise, and the controlling entity is called its parent (or the parent company.) The reason for this distinction is that a lone company cannot be a subsidiary of any organization; only an entity representing a legal fiction as a separate entity can be a subsidiary.
Job interview	A Job interview is a process in which a potential employee is evaluated by an employer for prospective employment in their company, organization and was established in the late 16th century. A Job interview typically precedes the hiring decision, and is used to evaluate the candidate. The interview is usually preceded by the evaluation of submitted résumés from interested candidates, then selecting a small number of candidates for interviews.

Profit	A profit , in the law of real property, is a nonpossessory interest in land similar to the better-known easement, which gives the holder the right to take natural resources such as petroleum, minerals, timber, and wild game from the land of another. Indeed, because of the necessity of allowing access to the land so that resources may be gathered, every profit contains an implied easement for the owner of the profit to enter the other party"s land for the purpose of collecting the resources permitted by the profit.
	Like an easement, profits can be created expressly by an agreement between the property owner and the owner of the profit, or by prescription, where the owner of the profit has made "open and notorious" use of the land for a continuous and uninterrupted statutory period.
Consideration	Consideration is the legal concept of value in connection with contracts. It is anything of value in the common sense, promised to another when making a contract. It can take the form of money, physical objects, services, promised actions, or even abstinence from a future action.
Contract	Agreement is said to be reached when an offer capable of immediate acceptance is met with a "mirror image" acceptance (ie, an unqualified acceptance). The parties must have the necessary capacity to Contract and the Contract must not be either trifling, indeterminate, impossible or illegal. Contract law is based on the principle expressed in the Latin phrase pacta sunt servanda .
Sale of goods	The sale of goods Act 1979 (c.54) is an Act of the Parliament of the United Kingdom which regulates contracts in which goods are sold and bought. The Act consolidates the sale of goods Act 1893 and subsequent legislation, which in turn consolidated the previous common law.
	The sale of goods Act performs several functions.
Cash	Two primary accounting methods, cash and accrual basis, are used to calculate taxable income for U.S. federal income taxes. According to the Internal Revenue Code, a taxpayer may compute taxable income by:
	· the cash receipts and disbursements method; · an accrual method; · any other method permitted by the chapter; or · any combination of the foregoing methods permitted under regulations prescribed by the Secretary. As a general rule, a taxpayer must compute taxable income using the same accounting method he uses to compute income in keeping his books.
Breach of contract	Breach of contract is a legal concept in which a binding agreement or bargained-for exchange is not honored by one or more of the parties to the contract by non-performance or interference with the other party"s performance.
	A minor breach, a partial breach or an immaterial breach, occurs when the non-breaching party is unentitled to an order for performance of its obligations, but only to collect the actual amount of their damages. For example, suppose a homeowner hires a contractor to install new plumbing and insists that the pipes, which will ultimately be sealed behind the walls, be red.

| Rules of origin | Rules of origin are used to determine the country of origin of a product for purposes of international trade. There are two common type of Rules of origin depending upon application, the preferential and non-preferential Rules of origin The exact rules vary from country to country. |

Age Discrimination in Employment Act	The Age Discrimination in Employment Act of 1967, Pub. L. No. 90-202, 81 Stat. 602 (Dec.
Contract	Agreement is said to be reached when an offer capable of immediate acceptance is met with a "mirror image" acceptance (ie, an unqualified acceptance). The parties must have the necessary capacity to Contract and the Contract must not be either trifling, indeterminate, impossible or illegal. Contract law is based on the principle expressed in the Latin phrase pacta sunt servanda .
Employment	Employment is a contract between two parties, one being the employer and the other being the employee. An employee may be defined as: "A person in the service of another under any contract of hire, express or implied, oral or written, where the employer has the power or right to control and direct the employee in the material details of how the work is to be performed." Black"s Law Dictionary page 471 (5th ed. 1979).
Ratification	Ratification is the act of approving and paying for supplies or services provided to and accepted by the government as a result of an unauthorized commitment. It gives official sanction or approval to a formal document such as a treaty or constitution. It includes the process of adopting an international treaty by the legislature, a constitution, or another nationally binding document (such as an amendment to a constitution) by the agreement of multiple sub-national entities.
Sale of Goods	The sale of goods Act 1979 (c.54) is an Act of the Parliament of the United Kingdom which regulates contracts in which goods are sold and bought. The Act consolidates the sale of goods Act 1893 and subsequent legislation, which in turn consolidated the previous common law. The sale of goods Act performs several functions.
World Intellectual Property Organization	The World Intellectual Property Organization is one of the 16 specialized agencies of the United Nations. World Intellectual Property Organization was created in 1967 "to encourage creative activity, to promote the protection of intellectual property throughout the world". World Intellectual Property Organization currently has 184 member states, administers 24 international treaties, and is headquartered in Geneva, Switzerland.
Business	There are many ways in which a business may be owned under the legal system of England and Wales. Different types of ownership are suitable for organisations depending on the degree of control the owners wish to have over the business. The choice of ownership methor also relates to the organisations ability to raise funds for the business activities.
Charter	A Charter is the grant of authority or rights, stating that the granter formally recognizes the prerogative of the recipient to exercise the rights specified. It is implicit that the granter retains superiority (or sovereignty), and that the recipient admits a limited (or inferior) status within the relationship, and it is within that sense that Charters were historically granted, and that sense is retained in modern usage of the term. Also, Charter can simply be a document giving royal permission to start a colony.

Forum selection clause	A Forum selection clause in a contract with a Conflict of Laws element allows the parties to agree that any litigation resulting from that contract will be initiated in a specific forum. There are three types of clause: · the reference might be to a particular court in a jurisdiction agreed upon by the parties (although, if the parties make a mistake as to the power of the nominated court to hear the matter, the civil procedures of the nominated jurisdiction will be applied to identify the appropriate court); or · the clause might refer to a specific kind of dispute resolution process, such as mediation, arbitration , or a hearing before a special referee; or · the clause might refer to both, requiring a specific process to be carried out in a specific location. The choice of law stage in a Conflict case requires the forum court to decide which of several competing laws should be applied to resolve the dispute.
Special Drawing Rights	Special Drawing Rights are potential claims on the freely usable currencies of International Monetary Fund members. Special Drawing Rights have the ISO 4217 currency code XDR. Special Drawing Rights are defined in terms of a basket of major currencies used in international trade and finance.
Competition law	Competition law, known in the United States as antitrust law, has three main elements: · prohibiting agreements or practices that restrict free trading and competition between business entities. This includes in particular the repression of cartels. · banning abusive behavior by a firm dominating a market, or anti-competitive practices that tend to lead to such a dominant position.
United Nations Convention on Contracts for the International Sale of Goods	The United Nations Convention on Contracts for the International Sale of Goods is a treaty offering a uniform international sales law that, as of July 2008, had been ratified by 71 countries that account for a significant proportion of world trade, making it one of the most successful international uniform laws. Japan is the most recent State to have ratified the Convention. It allows exporters to avoid choice of law issues as it offers "accepted substantive rules on which contracting parties, courts, and arbitrators may rely".
United Nations Commission on International Trade Law	The United Nations Commission on International Trade Law was established by the United Nations General Assembly by its Resolution 2205 (XXI) of 17 December 1966 "to promote the progressive harmonization and unification of international trade law. UNCITRAL carries out its work at annual sessions held alternately in New York City and Vienna. When world trade began to expand dramatically in the 1960s, national governments began to realize the need for a global set of standards and rules to harmonize national and regional regulations, which until then governed international trade.
Trademark	A trademark or trade mark is a distinctive sign or indicator used by an individual, business organization and to distinguish its products or services from those of other entities.

A trademark is designated by the following symbols:

· â„¢ (for an unregistered trademark that is, a mark used to promote or brand goods);
· â„ (for an unregistered service mark, that is, a mark used to promote or brand services); and
· Â® (for a registered trademark)

A trademark is a type of intellectual property, and typically a name, word, phrase, logo, symbol, design, image, or a combination of these elements. There is also a range of non-conventional trademark s comprising marks which do not fall into these standard categories.

The owner of a registered trademark may commence legal proceedings for trademark infringement to prevent unauthorized use of that trademark

World Bank	The World Bank is an international financial institution that provides financial and technical assistance to developing countries for development programs (e.g. bridges, roads, schools, etc.) with the stated goal of reducing poverty. The World Bank differs from the World Bank Group, in that the World Bank comprises only two institutions: · International Bank for Reconstruction and Development (IBRD) · International Development Association (IDA) Whereas the latter incorporates these two in addition to three more: · International Finance Corporation (IFC) · Multilateral Investment Guarantee Agency (MIGA) · International Centre for Settlement of Investment Disputes (ICSID) John Maynard Keynes (right) represented the UK at the conference, and Harry Dexter White represented the US. The World Bank is one of two major financial institutions created as a result of the Bretton Woods Conference in 1944. The International Monetary Fund, a related but separate institution, is the second.
Bribery	Bribery, a form of pecuniary corruption, is an act implying money or gift given that alters the behaviour of the recipient. Bribery constitutes a crime and is defined by Black"s Law Dictionary as the offering, giving, receiving, or soliciting of any item of value to influence the actions of an official or other person in discharge of a public or legal duty. The bribe is the gift bestowed to influence the recipient"s conduct.
Tariff	A Tariff is a duty imposed on goods when they are moved across a political boundary. They are usually associated with protectionism, the economic policy of restraining trade between nations. For political reasons, Tariff s are usually imposed on imported goods, although they may also be imposed on exported goods.
World Trade Organization	The World Trade Organization is an important selective, mainly private, international organization designed by its founders to supervise and liberalize international trade. The organization officially commenced on 1 January 1995, under the Marrakesh Agreement, succeeding the 1947 General Agreement on Tariffs and Trade (GATT.)

The World Trade Organization deals with regulation of trade between participating countries; it provides a framework for negotiating and formalising trade agreements, and a dispute resolution process aimed at enforcing participants" adherence to World Trade Organization agreements which are signed by representatives of member governments and ratified by their parliaments.

Numerary

Numerary is a civil designation for persons who are incorporated in a fixed or permanent way to a society or group: regular member of the working staff, permanent staff distinguished from a super Numerary .

The term Numerary and its counterpart, "super Numerary ," originated in Spanish and Latin American academy and government; it is now also used in countries all over the world, such as France, the U.S., England, Italy, etc.

There are Numerary members of surgical organizations, of universities, of gastronomical associations, etc.

Arbitration

Arbitration, a form of alternative dispute resolution (ADR), is a legal technique for the resolution of disputes outside the courts, wherein the parties to a dispute refer it to one or more persons (the "arbitrators", "arbiters" or "arbitral tribunal"), by whose decision (the "award") they agree to be bound. It is a settlement technique in which a third party reviews the case and imposes a decision that is legally binding for both sides. Other forms of ADR include mediation (a form of settlement negotiation facilitated by a neutral third party) and non-binding resolution by experts.

Statute

A statute is a formal written enactment of a legislative authority that governs a country, state, city, or county. Typically, statute s command or prohibit something, or declare policy. The word is often used to distinguish law made by legislative bodies from case law and the regulations issued by Government agencies.

Constitution

· Apostolic Constitution (a class of Roman Catholic Church documents)
· Constitution of the Roman Republic
· Constitutional court
· Constitutionalism
· Corporate Constitution
· Judicial activism
· Judicial restraint
· Judicial review
Judicial philosophies of Constitutional interpretation (note: generally specific to United States Constitutional law)

· List of national Constitutions
· Originalism
· Strict constructionism
· Textualism
· Proposed European Union Constitution

· Treaty of Lisbon (adopts same changes, but without Constitutional name)
· United Nations Charter

Sentencing Guidelines	The Federal Sentencing guidelines are rules that set out a uniform sentencing policy for convicted felons in the United States federal courts system. The Guidelines are the product of the United States Sentencing Commission and are part of an overall federal sentencing reform package that took effect in the mid-1960s. The implementation of this reform package was the result of bipartisan cooperation, led chiefly by Senator Edward Kennedy, as Chair of the Senate Judiciary Committee, and Attorney General Edwin Meese.
Tort	Tort law is a body of law that addresses, and provides remedies for, civil wrongs not arising out of contractual obligations. A person who suffers legal damages may be able to use Tort law to receive compensation from someone who is legally responsible, or "liable," for those injuries. Generally speaking, Tort law defines what constitutes a legal injury and establishes the circumstances under which one person may be held liable for another"s injury.
United States	

· History of competition law
· Monopoly

· Coercive monopoly
· Natural monopoly
· Barriers to entry
· Market power
· SSNIP test
· Relevant market
· Merger control

Anti-competitive practices

· Monopolization
· Collusion

· Formation of cartels
· Price fixing
· Bid rigging
· Product bundling and tying
· Refusal to deal

· Group boycott
· Exclusive dealing
· Dividing territories
· Conscious parallelism
· Predatory pricing
· Misuse of patents and copyrights

Laws and doctrines

United States

· Sherman Antitrust Act
· Clayton Antitrust Act
· Robinson-Patman Act
· FTC Act
· Hart-Scott-Rodino Act
· Merger guidelines
· Essential facilities doctrine
· Noerr-Pennington doctrine
· Parker immunity doctrine
· Rule of reason

Europe

· UK competition law
· Irish competition law

Australia

· Trade Practices Act 1974

Enforcement authorities and organizations

Competition law history refers to attempts by governments to regulate competitive markets for goods and services, leading up to the modern competition or antitrust laws around the world today. The earliest records traces back to the efforts of Roman legislators to control price fluctuations and unfair trade practices. Through the Middle Ages in Europe, Kings and Queens repeatedly cracked down on monopolies, including those created through state legislation.

· International Competition Network
· List of competition regulators

28

Arbitration	Arbitration, a form of alternative dispute resolution (ADR), is a legal technique for the resolution of disputes outside the courts, wherein the parties to a dispute refer it to one or more persons (the "arbitrators", "arbiters" or "arbitral tribunal"), by whose decision (the "award") they agree to be bound. It is a settlement technique in which a third party reviews the case and imposes a decision that is legally binding for both sides. Other forms of ADR include mediation (a form of settlement negotiation facilitated by a neutral third party) and non-binding resolution by experts.
Consideration	Consideration is the legal concept of value in connection with contracts. It is anything of value in the common sense, promised to another when making a contract. It can take the form of money, physical objects, services, promised actions, or even abstinence from a future action.
Bribery	Bribery, a form of pecuniary corruption, is an act implying money or gift given that alters the behaviour of the recipient. Bribery constitutes a crime and is defined by Black"s Law Dictionary as the offering, giving, receiving, or soliciting of any item of value to influence the actions of an official or other person in discharge of a public or legal duty. The bribe is the gift bestowed to influence the recipient"s conduct.
Federal Arbitration Act	In United States law, the Federal Arbitration Act is a statute that provides for judicial facilitation of private dispute resolution through arbitration. It applies in both state courts and federal courts, as was held in Southland v. Keating (although several Justices of the Supreme Court have admitted that Southland was wrongly decided and they would be willing to overrule it). It applies where the transaction contemplated by the parties "involves" interstate commerce and is predicated on an exercise of the "Commerce Clause" powers given to Congress in the U.S. Constitution.
Chief brand officer	A Chief brand officer is a relatively new executive level position at a corporation, company, organization typically reporting directly to the CEO or board of directors. The Chief brand officer is responsible for a brand"s image, experience, and promise, and propagating it throughout all aspects of the company. The brand officer oversees marketing, advertising, design, public relations and customer service departments.
Arbitration clause	An Arbitration clause is a commonly used clause in a contract that requires the parties to resolve their disputes through an arbitration process. Although such a clause may or may not specify that arbitration occur within a specific jurisdiction, it always binds the parties to a type of resolution outside of the courts, and is therefore considered a kind of forum selection clause. In the United States, the federal government has expressed a policy of support of Arbitration clauses, because they reduce the burden on court systems to resolve disputes.
Arbitration award	An Arbitration award (or arbitral award) is a determination on the merits by an arbitration tribunal in an arbitration, and is analogous to a judgment in a court of law. It is referred to as an "award" even where all of the claimant"s claims fail (and thus no money needs to be paid by either party), or the award is of a non-monetary nature. Although Arbitration awards are characteristically an award of damages against a party, tribunals usually have a range of remedies that can form a part of the award.

Constitution	
	· Apostolic Constitution (a class of Roman Catholic Church documents)
	· Constitution of the Roman Republic
	· Constitutional court
	· Constitutionalism
	· Corporate Constitution
	· Judicial activism
	· Judicial restraint
	· Judicial review
	Judicial philosophies of Constitutional interpretation (note: generally specific to United States Constitutional law)
	· List of national Constitutions
	· Originalism
	· Strict constructionism
	· Textualism
	· Proposed European Union Constitution
	· Treaty of Lisbon (adopts same changes, but without Constitutional name)
	· United Nations Charter
Terrorism	Terrorism is a policy or ideology of violence intended to intimidate or cause terror for the purpose of "exerting pressure on decision making by state bodies." The term "terror" is largely used to indicate clandestine, low-intensity violence that targets civilians and generates public fear. Thus "terror" is distinct from asymmetric warfare, and violates the concept of a common law of war in which civilian life is regarded. The term "-ism" is used to indicate an ideology --typically one that claims its attacks are in the domain of a "just war" concept, though most condemn such as crimes against humanity.
Service of process	Service of process is the procedure employed to give legal notice to a person (such as a defendant) of a court or administrative body"s exercise of its jurisdiction over that person so as to enable that person to respond to the proceeding before the court, body or other tribunal. Usually, notice is furnished by delivering a set of court documents (called "process") to the person to be served. Each jurisdiction has rules regarding the means of Service of process.
Business	There are many ways in which a business may be owned under the legal system of England and Wales. Different types of ownership are suitable for organisations depending on the degree of control the owners wish to have over the business. The choice of ownership methor also relates to the organisations ability to raise funds for the business activities.
Forum selection clause	A Forum selection clause in a contract with a Conflict of Laws element allows the parties to agree that any litigation resulting from that contract will be initiated in a specific forum. There are three types of clause:

· the reference might be to a particular court in a jurisdiction agreed upon by the parties (although, if the parties make a mistake as to the power of the nominated court to hear the matter, the civil procedures of the nominated jurisdiction will be applied to identify the appropriate court); or

· the clause might refer to a specific kind of dispute resolution process, such as mediation, arbitration , or a hearing before a special referee; or

· the clause might refer to both, requiring a specific process to be carried out in a specific location.

The choice of law stage in a Conflict case requires the forum court to decide which of several competing laws should be applied to resolve the dispute.

Contract

Agreement is said to be reached when an offer capable of immediate acceptance is met with a "mirror image" acceptance (ie, an unqualified acceptance). The parties must have the necessary capacity to Contract and the Contract must not be either trifling, indeterminate, impossible or illegal. Contract law is based on the principle expressed in the Latin phrase pacta sunt servanda .

Tort

Tort law is a body of law that addresses, and provides remedies for, civil wrongs not arising out of contractual obligations. A person who suffers legal damages may be able to use Tort law to receive compensation from someone who is legally responsible, or "liable," for those injuries. Generally speaking, Tort law defines what constitutes a legal injury and establishes the circumstances under which one person may be held liable for another"s injury.

Sale of Goods

The sale of goods Act 1979 (c.54) is an Act of the Parliament of the United Kingdom which regulates contracts in which goods are sold and bought. The Act consolidates the sale of goods Act 1893 and subsequent legislation, which in turn consolidated the previous common law.

The sale of goods Act performs several functions.

Contract	Agreement is said to be reached when an offer capable of immediate acceptance is met with a "mirror image" acceptance (ie, an unqualified acceptance). The parties must have the necessary capacity to Contract and the Contract must not be either trifling, indeterminate, impossible or illegal. Contract law is based on the principle expressed in the Latin phrase pacta sunt servanda .
Sale of Goods	The sale of goods Act 1979 (c.54) is an Act of the Parliament of the United Kingdom which regulates contracts in which goods are sold and bought. The Act consolidates the sale of goods Act 1893 and subsequent legislation, which in turn consolidated the previous common law. The sale of goods Act performs several functions.
Uniform Commercial Code	The Uniform Commercial Code is one of a number of uniform acts that have been promulgated in conjunction with efforts to harmonize the law of sales and other commercial transactions in all 50 states within the United States of America. This objective is deemed important because of the prevalence today of commercial transactions that extend beyond one state (for example, where the goods are manufactured in state A, warehoused in state B, sold from state C and delivered in state D.) The Uniform Commercial Code deals primarily with transactions involving personal property (movable property), not real property (immovable property.)
United States	· History of competition law · Monopoly

· Coercive monopoly
· Natural monopoly
· Barriers to entry
· Market power
· SSNIP test
· Relevant market
· Merger control

Anti-competitive practices

· Monopolization
· Collusion

· Formation of cartels
· Price fixing
· Bid rigging
· Product bundling and tying
· Refusal to deal

· Group boycott
· Exclusive dealing
· Dividing territories
· Conscious parallelism
· Predatory pricing
· Misuse of patents and copyrights

Laws and doctrines

United States

· Sherman Antitrust Act
· Clayton Antitrust Act
· Robinson-Patman Act
· FTC Act
· Hart-Scott-Rodino Act
· Merger guidelines
· Essential facilities doctrine
· Noerr-Pennington doctrine
· Parker immunity doctrine
· Rule of reason

Europe

· UK competition law
· Irish competition law

Australia

· Trade Practices Act 1974

Enforcement authorities and organizations

Competition law history refers to attempts by governments to regulate competitive markets for goods and services, leading up to the modern competition or antitrust laws around the world today. The earliest records traces back to the efforts of Roman legislators to control price fluctuations and unfair trade practices. Through the Middle Ages in Europe, Kings and Queens repeatedly cracked down on monopolies, including those created through state legislation.

· International Competition Network
· List of competition regulators

Forum selection clause

A Forum selection clause in a contract with a Conflict of Laws element allows the parties to agree that any litigation resulting from that contract will be initiated in a specific forum. There are three types of clause:

· the reference might be to a particular court in a jurisdiction agreed upon by the parties (although, if the parties make a mistake as to the power of the nominated court to hear the matter, the civil procedures of the nominated jurisdiction will be applied to identify the appropriate court); or
· the clause might refer to a specific kind of dispute resolution process, such as mediation, arbitration , or a hearing before a special referee; or
· the clause might refer to both, requiring a specific process to be carried out in a specific location.
The choice of law stage in a Conflict case requires the forum court to decide which of several competing laws should be applied to resolve the dispute.

Choice of law clause	A Choice of law clause or proper law clause in a contract is one in which the parties specify which law (i.e. the law of which state or nation if it only has a single legal system) will be applied to resolve any disputes arising under the contract. If all the parties and the relevant factual elements affecting formation, validity, and performance are geographically located in the same state, it will be obvious that, if the contract is silent on the point, the local municipal law (usually called the lex loci contractus, i.e. the law of the place where the contract was made) will be applied as the law governing substantive issues. The lex fori, i.e. the law of the local forum court, will be applied to procedural matters (such as evidentiary rules, etc).
Arbitration	Arbitration, a form of alternative dispute resolution (ADR), is a legal technique for the resolution of disputes outside the courts, wherein the parties to a dispute refer it to one or more persons (the "arbitrators", "arbiters" or "arbitral tribunal"), by whose decision (the "award") they agree to be bound. It is a settlement technique in which a third party reviews the case and imposes a decision that is legally binding for both sides. Other forms of ADR include mediation (a form of settlement negotiation facilitated by a neutral third party) and non-binding resolution by experts.
Breach of contract	Breach of contract is a legal concept in which a binding agreement or bargained-for exchange is not honored by one or more of the parties to the contract by non-performance or interference with the other party"s performance. A minor breach, a partial breach or an immaterial breach, occurs when the non-breaching party is unentitled to an order for performance of its obligations, but only to collect the actual amount of their damages. For example, suppose a homeowner hires a contractor to install new plumbing and insists that the pipes, which will ultimately be sealed behind the walls, be red.
United Nations Commission on International Trade Law	The United Nations Commission on International Trade Law was established by the United Nations General Assembly by its Resolution 2205 (XXI) of 17 December 1966 "to promote the progressive harmonization and unification of international trade law. UNCITRAL carries out its work at annual sessions held alternately in New York City and Vienna. When world trade began to expand dramatically in the 1960s, national governments began to realize the need for a global set of standards and rules to harmonize national and regional regulations, which until then governed international trade.

World Intellectual Property Organization	The World Intellectual Property Organization is one of the 16 specialized agencies of the United Nations. World Intellectual Property Organization was created in 1967 "to encourage creative activity, to promote the protection of intellectual property throughout the world". World Intellectual Property Organization currently has 184 member states, administers 24 international treaties, and is headquartered in Geneva, Switzerland.
Business	There are many ways in which a business may be owned under the legal system of England and Wales. Different types of ownership are suitable for organisations depending on the degree of control the owners wish to have over the business. The choice of ownership methor also relates to the organisations ability to raise funds for the business activities.
Ratification	Ratification is the act of approving and paying for supplies or services provided to and accepted by the government as a result of an unauthorized commitment. It gives official sanction or approval to a formal document such as a treaty or constitution. It includes the process of adopting an international treaty by the legislature, a constitution, or another nationally binding document (such as an amendment to a constitution) by the agreement of multiple sub-national entities.
Tariff	A Tariff is a duty imposed on goods when they are moved across a political boundary. They are usually associated with protectionism, the economic policy of restraining trade between nations. For political reasons, Tariff s are usually imposed on imported goods, although they may also be imposed on exported goods.
Valid	The term valid ity in logic applies to arguments or statements. An argument is valid if and only if the truth of its premises entails the truth of its conclusion, it would be self-contradictory to affirm the premises and deny the conclusion. The corresponding conditional of a valid argument is a logical truth and the negation of its corresponding conditional is a contradiction.
Validity	The term validity in logic applies to arguments or statements. An argument is valid if and only if the truth of its premises entails the truth of its conclusion, it would be self-contradictory to affirm the premises and deny the conclusion. The corresponding conditional of a valid argument is a logical truth and the negation of its corresponding conditional is a contradiction.
Parol evidence	The Parol evidence rule is the legal application of a rule of substantive law in contract cases that prevents a party to a written contract from contradicting (or sometimes adding to) the terms of the contract by seeking the admission of evidence "extrinsic" (outside) to the contract. For example, Carl agrees in writing to sell Betty a car for $1,000. Betty argues that Carl told her that she would only need to pay Carl $800.

Parol evidence rule	The Parol evidence rule is the legal application of a rule of substantive law in contract cases that prevents a party to a written contract from contradicting (or sometimes adding to) the terms of the contract by seeking the admission of evidence "extrinsic" (outside) to the contract. For example, Carl agrees in writing to sell Betty a car for $1,000. Betty argues that Carl told her that she would only need to pay Carl $800.
Excuse	In jurisprudence, an Excuse or justification is a defense to criminal charges that is distinct from an exculpation. In this context, "to Excuse" means to grant or obtain an exemption for a group of persons sharing a common characteristic from a potential liability. "To justify" as in justifiable homicide means to "vindicate" or show the justice in the particular conduct.
Job interview	A Job interview is a process in which a potential employee is evaluated by an employer for prospective employment in their company, organization and was established in the late 16th century. A Job interview typically precedes the hiring decision, and is used to evaluate the candidate. The interview is usually preceded by the evaluation of submitted résumés from interested candidates, then selecting a small number of candidates for interviews.
Firm offer	In the United States, a Firm offer allows merchants to make offers to buy or sell irrevocable for up to three months provided that the offer be put down in writing or otherwise authenticated. Such offers are defined by UCC Â§ 2-205 of the Uniform Commercial Code of the United States. A Firm offer in effect creates an option contract without requiring any consideration from the prospective buyer.
Mirror image rule	In the law of contracts, the Mirror image rule, also referred to as an unequivocal and absolute acceptance requirement states that an offer must be accepted exactly without modifications. The offeror is the master of his own offer. An attempt to accept the offer on different terms instead creates a counter-offer, and this constitutes a rejection of the original offer.
OPIC	The OPIC (OPIC) is an agency of the United States Government established in 1971 that helps U.S. businesses invest overseas and promotes economic development in new and emerging markets. OPIC"s mission is to "foster economic development in new and emerging markets, support U.S. foreign policy and create U.S. jobs by helping U.S. businesses to invest overseas." The agency provides political risk insurance against the risks of inconvertibility, political violence, or expropriation. OPIC also provides financing through direct loans and loan guarantees.
Overseas Private Investment Corporation	The Overseas Private Investment Corporation is an agency of the United States Government established in 1971 that helps U.S. businesses invest overseas and promotes economic development in new and emerging markets. Overseas Private Investment Corporation"s mission is to "foster economic development in new and emerging markets, support U.S. foreign policy and create U.S. jobs by helping U.S. businesses to invest overseas." The agency provides political risk insurance against the risks of inconvertibility, political violence, or expropriation. Overseas Private Investment Corporation also provides financing through direct loans and loan guarantees.

Chapter 4. Sales Contracts and Excuses for Nonperformance

United Nations Convention on Contracts for the International Sale of Goods	The United Nations Convention on Contracts for the International Sale of Goods is a treaty offering a uniform international sales law that, as of July 2008, had been ratified by 71 countries that account for a significant proportion of world trade, making it one of the most successful international uniform laws. Japan is the most recent State to have ratified the Convention.

It allows exporters to avoid choice of law issues as it offers "accepted substantive rules on which contracting parties, courts, and arbitrators may rely". |
| Warranty | In commercial and consumer transactions, a warranty is an obligation or guarantee that an article or service sold is as factually stated or legally implied by the seller, and that often provides for a specific remedy such as repair or replacement in the event the article or service fails to meet the warranty. A breach of warranty occurs when the promise is broken, i.e., a product is defective or not as should be expected by a reasonable buyer.

In business and legal transactions, a warranty is an assurance by one party to the other party that certain facts or conditions are true or will happen; the other party is permitted to rely on that assurance and seek some type of remedy if it is not true or followed. |
| Fundamental breach | A Fundamental breach of a contract, sometimes known as a repudiatory breach, is a breach so fundamental that it permits the distressed party to terminate performance of the contract, in addition to entitling that party to sue for damages.

The law of Fundamental breach was historically treated as an extension of the doctrine of deviation. The development of this doctrine can be traced down to the first half of the 19th century, when Tindal C.J. stated in Davis v. Garrett that deviation made by the carrier from the agreed voyage route brings the latter outside of contract and therefore outside of exceptions or limitation clauses provided by such a contract. |
Liquidation	In law, Liquidation refers to the process by which a company (or part of a company) is brought to an end, and the assets and property of the company redistributed. Liquidation can also be referred to as winding-up or dissolution, although dissolution technically refers to the last stage of Liquidation. The process of Liquidation also arises when customs, an authority or agency in a country responsible for collecting and safeguarding customs duties, determines the final computation or ascertainment of the duties or drawback accruing on an entry.
Damages	Damages for breach of contract is a common law remedy, available as of right. It is designed to compensate the victim for their actual loss as a result of the wrongdoer"s breach rather than to punish the wrongdoer. If no loss has been occasioned by the plaintiff, only nominal Damages will be awarded.
Contract price	A Contract price is the price listed in the contract for the good or services to be received in return. In contract law, the Contract price is a material term. The Contract price as the price for the good or services to be received in the contract determines whether a contract may exist.

Profit	A profit , in the law of real property, is a nonpossessory interest in land similar to the better-known easement, which gives the holder the right to take natural resources such as petroleum, minerals, timber, and wild game from the land of another. Indeed, because of the necessity of allowing access to the land so that resources may be gathered, every profit contains an implied easement for the owner of the profit to enter the other party"s land for the purpose of collecting the resources permitted by the profit. Like an easement, profits can be created expressly by an agreement between the property owner and the owner of the profit, or by prescription, where the owner of the profit has made "open and notorious" use of the land for a continuous and uninterrupted statutory period.
Specific performance	In the law of Remedy, an order of specific performance is an order of the court which requires a party to perform a specific act, usually what is stated in a contract. While specific performance can be in the form of any type of forced action, it is usually used to complete a previously established transaction, thus being the most effective remedy in protecting the expectation interest of the innocent party to a contract. It is usually the opposite of a prohibitory injunction but there are mandatory injunctions which have a similar effect to specific performance.
Frustration of purpose	In the law of contracts, Frustration of purpose is a defense to enforcement of the contract. Frustration of purpose occurs when an unforeseen event undermines a party"s principal purpose for entering into a contract, and both parties knew of this principal purpose at the time the contract was made. Despite frequently arising as a result of government action, any third party (or even nature) can frustrate a contracting party"s primary purpose for entering into the contract.
Impossibility	In contract law, Impossibility is an excuse for the nonperformance of duties under a contract, based on a change in circumstances (or the discovery of preexisting circumstances), the nonoccurrence of which was an underlying assumption of the contract, that makes performance of the contract literally impossible. For such a defense to be raised, performance must not merely be difficult or unexpectedly costly for one party; there must be no way for it to actually be accomplished. For example, if Rachel contracts to pay Joey $1000 to paint her house on October 1, but the house burns to the ground before the end of September, Rachel is excused from her duty to pay Joey the $1000, and he is excused from his duty to paint her house; however, Joey may still be able to sue for the unjust enrichment of any benefit conferred on Rachel before her house burned down.
United Nations Conference on Trade and Development	The United Nations Conference on Trade and Development was established in 1964 as a permanent intergovernmental body. It is the principal organ of the United Nations General Assembly dealing with trade, investment and development issues. The organization"s goals are to "maximize the trade, investment and development opportunities of developing countries and assist them in their efforts to integrate into the world economy on an equitable basis." (from official website.)

Impracticability	The doctrine of Impracticability in the common law of contracts excuses performance of a duty, where that duty has become unfeasibly difficult or expensive for the party who was to perform. It is similar in some respects to the doctrine of impossibility because it is triggered by the occurrence of a condition, the nonoccurrence of which was a basic assumption of the contract. The major difference between impossibility and Impracticability, however, is that while impossibility excuses performance where the contractual duty cannot physically be performed, the doctrine of Impracticability comes into play where performance is still physically possible, but would be very burdensome for the party whose performance is due.
Force majeure	Force majeure is a common clause in contracts which essentially frees both parties from liability or obligation when an extraordinary event or circumstance beyond the control of the parties, such as a war, strike, riot, crime prevents one or both parties from fulfilling their obligations under the contract. However, Force majeure is not intended to excuse negligence or other malfeasance of a party, as where non-performance is caused by the usual and natural consequences of external forces either when they become likely or when they actually occur.
Consideration	Consideration is the legal concept of value in connection with contracts. It is anything of value in the common sense, promised to another when making a contract. It can take the form of money, physical objects, services, promised actions, or even abstinence from a future action.

Sale of goods	The sale of goods Act 1979 (c.54) is an Act of the Parliament of the United Kingdom which regulates contracts in which goods are sold and bought. The Act consolidates the sale of goods Act 1893 and subsequent legislation, which in turn consolidated the previous common law. The sale of goods Act performs several functions.
Cash	Two primary accounting methods, cash and accrual basis, are used to calculate taxable income for U.S. federal income taxes. According to the Internal Revenue Code, a taxpayer may compute taxable income by: · the cash receipts and disbursements method; · an accrual method; · any other method permitted by the chapter; or · any combination of the foregoing methods permitted under regulations prescribed by the Secretary. As a general rule, a taxpayer must compute taxable income using the same accounting method he uses to compute income in keeping his books.
Contract	Agreement is said to be reached when an offer capable of immediate acceptance is met with a "mirror image" acceptance (ie, an unqualified acceptance). The parties must have the necessary capacity to Contract and the Contract must not be either trifling, indeterminate, impossible or illegal. Contract law is based on the principle expressed in the Latin phrase pacta sunt servanda .
Negotiable instrument	A Negotiable instrument is a specialized type of "contract" for the payment of money that is unconditional and capable of transfer by negotiation. Common examples include cheques, banknotes (paper money), and commercial paper. A Negotiable instrument is not a contract, as contract formation requires an offer, acceptance, and consideration, none of which is an element of a Negotiable instrument.
Uniform Commercial Code	The Uniform Commercial Code is one of a number of uniform acts that have been promulgated in conjunction with efforts to harmonize the law of sales and other commercial transactions in all 50 states within the United States of America. This objective is deemed important because of the prevalence today of commercial transactions that extend beyond one state (for example, where the goods are manufactured in state A, warehoused in state B, sold from state C and delivered in state D.) The Uniform Commercial Code deals primarily with transactions involving personal property (movable property), not real property (immovable property.)
Bill of lading	A Bill of lading (sometimes referred to as a Bill of lading,or B/L) is a document issued by a carrier to a shipper, acknowledging that specified goods have been received on board as cargo for conveyance to a named place for delivery to the consignee who is usually identified. A through Bill of lading involves the use of at least two different modes of transport from road, rail, air, and sea. The term derives from the noun "bill", a schedule of costs for services supplied or to be supplied, and from the verb "to lade" which means to load a cargo onto a ship or other form of transport.
Guarantee	The act of becoming a surety is also called a Guarantee. Traditionally a Guarantee was distinguished from a surety in that the surety"s liability was joint and primary with the principal, whereas the guaranty"s liability was ancillary and derivative, but many jurisdictions have abolished this distinction

Lien	In law, a Lien is a form of security interest granted over an item of property to secure the payment of a debt or performance of some other obligation. The owner of the property, who grants the Lien, is referred to as the Lienor and the person who has the benefit of the Lien is referred to as the Lienee. The etymological root is Anglo-French Lien, loyen bond, restraint, from Latin ligamen, from ligare to bind.
Duty	Duty (from "due," that which is owing, O. Fr. deu, did, past participle of devoir; Lat. debere, debitum; cf.
Damages	Damages for breach of contract is a common law remedy, available as of right. It is designed to compensate the victim for their actual loss as a result of the wrongdoer"s breach rather than to punish the wrongdoer. If no loss has been occasioned by the plaintiff, only nominal Damages will be awarded.
Breach of contract	Breach of contract is a legal concept in which a binding agreement or bargained-for exchange is not honored by one or more of the parties to the contract by non-performance or interference with the other party"s performance. A minor breach, a partial breach or an immaterial breach, occurs when the non-breaching party is unentitled to an order for performance of its obligations, but only to collect the actual amount of their damages. For example, suppose a homeowner hires a contractor to install new plumbing and insists that the pipes, which will ultimately be sealed behind the walls, be red.
Reasonable care	In tort law, a duty of care is a legal obligation imposed on an individual requiring that they adhere to a standard of reasonable care while performing any acts that could foreseeably harm others. It is the first element that must be established to proceed with an action in negligence. The plaintiff must be able to articulate a duty of care imposed by law which the defendant has breached.
Consignee	In a contract of carriage, the Consignee is the person to whom the shipment is to be delivered whether by land, sea or air. This is a difficult area of law in that it regulates the mass transportation industry which cannot always guarantee arrival on time or that goods will not be damaged in the course of transit. A further two problems are that unpaid consignors or freight carriers may wish to hold goods until payment is made, and fraudulent individuals may seek to take delivery in place of the legitimate Consignees.
Warsaw Convention	The Warsaw Convention is an international convention which regulates liability for international carriage of persons, luggage or goods performed by aircraft for reward. Originally signed in 1929 in Warsaw (hence the name), it was amended in 1955 at The Hague and in 1975 in Montreal. United States courts have held that, at least for some purposes, the Warsaw Convention is a different instrument from the Warsaw Convention as Amended by the Hague Protocol.
Risk of loss	Risk of loss is a term used in the law of contracts to determine which party should bear the burden of risk for damage occurring to goods after the sale has been completed, but before delivery has occurred. Such considerations generally come into play after the contract is formed but before buyer receives goods, something bad happens.

There are four risk of loss rules, in order of application:

- · Agreement - the agreement of the parties controls
- · Breach - the breaching party is liable for any uninsured loss even though breach is unrelated to the problem. Hence, if the breach is the time of delivery, and the goods show up broken, then the breaching rule applies risk of loss on the seller.
- · Delivery by common carrier other than by seller.

  - · risk of loss shifts from seller to buyer at the time that seller completes its delivery obligations
  - · If it is a destination contract (FOB (buyer"s city)), then risk of loss is on the seller.
  - · If it is a delivery contract (standard, or FOB (seller"s city)), then the risk of loss is on the buyer.

- · If the seller is a merchant, then the risk of loss shifts to the buyer upon buyer"s "receipt" of the goods. If the buyer never takes possession, then the seller still has the risk of loss.

| North American Free Trade Agreement | The North American Free Trade Agreement is a trilateral trade bloc in North America created by the governments of the United States, Canada, and Mexico. The agreement creating the trade bloc came into force on January 1, 1994. It superseded the Canada-United States Free Trade Agreement between the U.S. and Canada. |

Consignee	In a contract of carriage, the Consignee is the person to whom the shipment is to be delivered whether by land, sea or air.
	This is a difficult area of law in that it regulates the mass transportation industry which cannot always guarantee arrival on time or that goods will not be damaged in the course of transit. A further two problems are that unpaid consignors or freight carriers may wish to hold goods until payment is made, and fraudulent individuals may seek to take delivery in place of the legitimate Consignees.
Chief brand officer	A Chief brand officer is a relatively new executive level position at a corporation, company, organization typically reporting directly to the CEO or board of directors. The Chief brand officer is responsible for a brand"s image, experience, and promise, and propagating it throughout all aspects of the company. The brand officer oversees marketing, advertising, design, public relations and customer service departments.
Contract	Agreement is said to be reached when an offer capable of immediate acceptance is met with a "mirror image" acceptance (ie, an unqualified acceptance). The parties must have the necessary capacity to Contract and the Contract must not be either trifling, indeterminate, impossible or illegal. Contract law is based on the principle expressed in the Latin phrase pacta sunt servanda .
Special Drawing Rights	Special Drawing Rights are potential claims on the freely usable currencies of International Monetary Fund members. Special Drawing Rights have the ISO 4217 currency code XDR.
	Special Drawing Rights are defined in terms of a basket of major currencies used in international trade and finance.
Warsaw Convention	The Warsaw Convention is an international convention which regulates liability for international carriage of persons, luggage or goods performed by aircraft for reward.
	Originally signed in 1929 in Warsaw (hence the name), it was amended in 1955 at The Hague and in 1975 in Montreal. United States courts have held that, at least for some purposes, the Warsaw Convention is a different instrument from the Warsaw Convention as Amended by the Hague Protocol.
Breach of contract	Breach of contract is a legal concept in which a binding agreement or bargained-for exchange is not honored by one or more of the parties to the contract by non-performance or interference with the other party"s performance.
	A minor breach, a partial breach or an immaterial breach, occurs when the non-breaching party is unentitled to an order for performance of its obligations, but only to collect the actual amount of their damages. For example, suppose a homeowner hires a contractor to install new plumbing and insists that the pipes, which will ultimately be sealed behind the walls, be red.
Himalaya clause	A Himalaya clause is a contractual provision expressed to be for the benefit of a third party who is not a party to the contract. Although theoretically applicable to any form of contract, most of the jurisprudence relating to Himalaya clauses relate to marine matters, and exclusion clauses in bills of lading for the benefit of stevedores in particular.
	The clause takes its name from a decision of the English Court of Appeal in the case of Adler v Dickson 2 Lloyd"s Rep 267, 1 QB 158 .

Forum selection clause	A Forum selection clause in a contract with a Conflict of Laws element allows the parties to agree that any litigation resulting from that contract will be initiated in a specific forum. There are three types of clause:
	· the reference might be to a particular court in a jurisdiction agreed upon by the parties (although, if the parties make a mistake as to the power of the nominated court to hear the matter, the civil procedures of the nominated jurisdiction will be applied to identify the appropriate court); or
	· the clause might refer to a specific kind of dispute resolution process, such as mediation, arbitration , or a hearing before a special referee; or
	· the clause might refer to both, requiring a specific process to be carried out in a specific location.
	The choice of law stage in a Conflict case requires the forum court to decide which of several competing laws should be applied to resolve the dispute.
Due diligence	Due diligence is a term used for a number of concepts involving either the performance of an investigation of a business or person, or the performance of an act with a certain standard of care. It can be a legal obligation, but the term will more commonly apply to voluntary investigations. A common example of Due diligence in various industries is the process through which a potential acquirer evaluates a target company or its assets for acquisition.
Terrorism	Terrorism is a policy or ideology of violence intended to intimidate or cause terror for the purpose of "exerting pressure on decision making by state bodies." The term "terror" is largely used to indicate clandestine, low-intensity violence that targets civilians and generates public fear. Thus "terror" is distinct from asymmetric warfare, and violates the concept of a common law of war in which civilian life is regarded. The term "-ism" is used to indicate an ideology --typically one that claims its attacks are in the domain of a "just war" concept, though most condemn such as crimes against humanity.
Power of attorney	A power of attorney or letter of attorney in common law systems or mandate in civil law systems is an authorization to act on someone else"s behalf in a legal or business matter. The person authorizing the other to act is the principal, granter or donor (of the power), and the one authorized to act is the agent, the attorney-in-fact, or in many Common Law jurisdictions, simply the attorney.
	The term attorney-in-fact is commonly used in the United States, to make a distinction from the term Attorney at law.
WTO	The WTO (WTO) is an international organization designed by its founders to supervise and liberalize international trade. The organization officially commenced on 1 January 1995, under the Marrakesh Agreement, succeeding the 1947 General Agreement on Tariffs and Trade (GATT.)
	The WTO deals with regulation of trade between participating countries; it provides a framework for negotiating and formalising trade agreements, and a dispute resolution process aimed at enforcing participants" adherence to WTO agreements which are signed by representatives of member governments and ratified by their parliaments.

Negotiable Instrument	A Negotiable instrument is a specialized type of "contract" for the payment of money that is unconditional and capable of transfer by negotiation. Common examples include cheques, banknotes (paper money), and commercial paper. A Negotiable instrument is not a contract, as contract formation requires an offer, acceptance, and consideration, none of which is an element of a Negotiable instrument.
Promissory Note	A promissory note, referred to as a note payable in accounting, just a "note" is a contract where one party (the maker or issuer) makes an unconditional promise in writing to pay a sum of money to the other (the payee), either at a fixed or determinable future time or on demand of the payee, under specific terms. They differ from IOUs in that they contain a specific promise to pay, rather than simply acknowledging that a debt exists. The terms of a note typically include the principal amount, the interest rate if any, the parties, the date, the terms of repayment (which could include interest) and the maturity date.
Promissory Notes	The terms of a note typically include the principal amount, the interest rate if any, and the maturity date. Sometimes, provisions are included concerning the payee"s rights in the event of a default, which may include foreclosure of the maker"s assets. Demand promissory Notes are notes that do not carry a specific maturity date, but are due on demand of the lender.
Sight draft	A draft can require immediate payment by the second party to the third upon presentation of the draft. This is called a Sight draft Cheques are Sight draft s.
USA PATRIOT Act	The USA Patriot Act, commonly known as the "Patriot Act", is a statute enacted by the United States Government that President George W. Bush signed into law on October 26, 2001. The contrived acronym stands for Uniting and Strengthening America by Providing Appropriate Tools Required to Intercept and Obstruct Terrorism Act of 2001 (Public Law Pub.L. 107-56.)
Uniform Commercial Code	The Uniform Commercial Code is one of a number of uniform acts that have been promulgated in conjunction with efforts to harmonize the law of sales and other commercial transactions in all 50 states within the United States of America. This objective is deemed important because of the prevalence today of commercial transactions that extend beyond one state (for example, where the goods are manufactured in state A, warehoused in state B, sold from state C and delivered in state D.) The Uniform Commercial Code deals primarily with transactions involving personal property (movable property), not real property (immovable property.)
Cash	Two primary accounting methods, cash and accrual basis, are used to calculate taxable income for U.S. federal income taxes. According to the Internal Revenue Code, a taxpayer may compute taxable income by: · the cash receipts and disbursements method; · an accrual method; · any other method permitted by the chapter; or · any combination of the foregoing methods permitted under regulations prescribed by the Secretary. As a general rule, a taxpayer must compute taxable income using the same accounting method he uses to compute income in keeping his books.

63

Contract	Agreement is said to be reached when an offer capable of immediate acceptance is met with a "mirror image" acceptance (ie, an unqualified acceptance). The parties must have the necessary capacity to Contract and the Contract must not be either trifling, indeterminate, impossible or illegal. Contract law is based on the principle expressed in the Latin phrase pacta sunt servanda .
Sale of goods	The sale of goods Act 1979 (c.54) is an Act of the Parliament of the United Kingdom which regulates contracts in which goods are sold and bought. The Act consolidates the sale of goods Act 1893 and subsequent legislation, which in turn consolidated the previous common law. The sale of goods Act performs several functions.
Revocation	Revocation is the act of recall or annulment. It is the reversal of an act, the recalling of a grant, or the making void of some deed previously existing. In the law of contracts, revocation is a type of remedy for buyers when the buyer accepts a nonconforming good from the seller.
Chief brand officer	A Chief brand officer is a relatively new executive level position at a corporation, company, organization typically reporting directly to the CEO or board of directors. The Chief brand officer is responsible for a brand"s image, experience, and promise, and propagating it throughout all aspects of the company. The brand officer oversees marketing, advertising, design, public relations and customer service departments.

United States

· History of competition law
· Monopoly

· Coercive monopoly
· Natural monopoly
· Barriers to entry
· Market power
· SSNIP test
· Relevant market
· Merger control

Anti-competitive practices

· Monopolization
· Collusion

· Formation of cartels
· Price fixing
· Bid rigging
· Product bundling and tying
· Refusal to deal

· Group boycott
· Exclusive dealing
· Dividing territories
· Conscious parallelism
· Predatory pricing
· Misuse of patents and copyrights

Laws and doctrines

United States

· Sherman Antitrust Act
· Clayton Antitrust Act
· Robinson-Patman Act
· FTC Act
· Hart-Scott-Rodino Act
· Merger guidelines
· Essential facilities doctrine
· Noerr-Pennington doctrine
· Parker immunity doctrine
· Rule of reason

Europe

· UK competition law
· Irish competition law

Australia

· Trade Practices Act 1974

Enforcement authorities and organizations

Competition law history refers to attempts by governments to regulate competitive markets for goods and services, leading up to the modern competition or antitrust laws around the world today. The earliest records traces back to the efforts of Roman legislators to control price fluctuations and unfair trade practices. Through the Middle Ages in Europe, Kings and Queens repeatedly cracked down on monopolies, including those created through state legislation.

· International Competition Network
· List of competition regulators

Tariff

A Tariff is a duty imposed on goods when they are moved across a political boundary. They are usually associated with protectionism, the economic policy of restraining trade between nations. For political reasons, Tariff s are usually imposed on imported goods, although they may also be imposed on exported goods.

North American Free Trade Agreement

The North American Free Trade Agreement is a trilateral trade bloc in North America created by the governments of the United States, Canada, and Mexico. The agreement creating the trade bloc came into force on January 1, 1994. It superseded the Canada-United States Free Trade Agreement between the U.S. and Canada.

| Separation of powers | The separation of powers is a model for the governance of democratic states. The model was first developed in ancient Greece and came into widespread use by the Roman Republic as part of the uncodified Constitution of the Roman Republic. Under this model, the state is divided into branches or estates, each with separate and independent powers and areas of responsibility. |

| United States | |

· History of competition law
· Monopoly

  · Coercive monopoly
  · Natural monopoly
  · Barriers to entry
  · Market power
  · SSNIP test
  · Relevant market
  · Merger control

Anti-competitive practices

· Monopolization
· Collusion

· Formation of cartels
· Price fixing
· Bid rigging
· Product bundling and tying
· Refusal to deal

  · Group boycott
  · Exclusive dealing
  · Dividing territories
  · Conscious parallelism
  · Predatory pricing
  · Misuse of patents and copyrights

Laws and doctrines

United States

· Sherman Antitrust Act
· Clayton Antitrust Act
· Robinson-Patman Act
· FTC Act
· Hart-Scott-Rodino Act
· Merger guidelines
· Essential facilities doctrine
· Noerr-Pennington doctrine
· Parker immunity doctrine
· Rule of reason

Europe

· UK competition law
· Irish competition law

Australia

· Trade Practices Act 1974

Enforcement authorities and organizations

Competition law history refers to attempts by governments to regulate competitive markets for goods and services, leading up to the modern competition or antitrust laws around the world today. The earliest records traces back to the efforts of Roman legislators to control price fluctuations and unfair trade practices. Through the Middle Ages in Europe, Kings and Queens repeatedly cracked down on monopolies, including those created through state legislation.

· International Competition Network
· List of competition regulators

Charter	A Charter is the grant of authority or rights, stating that the granter formally recognizes the prerogative of the recipient to exercise the rights specified. It is implicit that the granter retains superiority (or sovereignty), and that the recipient admits a limited (or inferior) status within the relationship, and it is within that sense that Charters were historically granted, and that sense is retained in modern usage of the term. Also, Charter can simply be a document giving royal permission to start a colony.
Supremacy clause	The Supremacy clause is a clause in the United States Constitution, article VI, paragraph 2. The clause establishes the Constitution, Federal Statutes, and U.S. treaties as "the supreme law of the land". The text establishes these as the highest form of law in the American legal system, mandating that state judges uphold them, even if state laws or constitutions conflict.
Warsaw Convention	The Warsaw Convention is an international convention which regulates liability for international carriage of persons, luggage or goods performed by aircraft for reward. Originally signed in 1929 in Warsaw (hence the name), it was amended in 1955 at The Hague and in 1975 in Montreal. United States courts have held that, at least for some purposes, the Warsaw Convention is a different instrument from the Warsaw Convention as Amended by the Hague Protocol.
Chief brand officer	A Chief brand officer is a relatively new executive level position at a corporation, company, organization typically reporting directly to the CEO or board of directors. The Chief brand officer is responsible for a brand"s image, experience, and promise, and propagating it throughout all aspects of the company. The brand officer oversees marketing, advertising, design, public relations and customer service departments.

Constitution	· Apostolic Constitution (a class of Roman Catholic Church documents) · Constitution of the Roman Republic · Constitutional court · Constitutionalism · Corporate Constitution · Judicial activism · Judicial restraint · Judicial review Judicial philosophies of Constitutional interpretation (note: generally specific to United States Constitutional law) · List of national Constitutions · Originalism · Strict constructionism · Textualism · Proposed European Union Constitution · Treaty of Lisbon (adopts same changes, but without Constitutional name) · United Nations Charter
Tariff	A Tariff is a duty imposed on goods when they are moved across a political boundary. They are usually associated with protectionism, the economic policy of restraining trade between nations. For political reasons, Tariff s are usually imposed on imported goods, although they may also be imposed on exported goods.
North American Free Trade Agreement	The North American Free Trade Agreement is a trilateral trade bloc in North America created by the governments of the United States, Canada, and Mexico. The agreement creating the trade bloc came into force on January 1, 1994. It superseded the Canada-United States Free Trade Agreement between the U.S. and Canada.
World Trade Organization	The World Trade Organization is an important selective, mainly private, international organization designed by its founders to supervise and liberalize international trade. The organization officially commenced on 1 January 1995, under the Marrakesh Agreement, succeeding the 1947 General Agreement on Tariffs and Trade (GATT.) The World Trade Organization deals with regulation of trade between participating countries; it provides a framework for negotiating and formalising trade agreements, and a dispute resolution process aimed at enforcing participants" adherence to World Trade Organization agreements which are signed by representatives of member governments and ratified by their parliaments.
Trading with the Enemy Act	The Trading with the Enemy Act, sometimes abbreviated as TWEA, is a United States federal law, 12 U.S.C. § 95a, enacted in 1917 to restrict trade with countries hostile to the United States. The law gives the President the power to oversee or restrict any and all trade between the U.S. and her enemies in times of war.

USA Patriot Act	The USA Patriot Act, commonly known as the "Patriot Act", is a statute enacted by the United States Government that President George W. Bush signed into law on October 26, 2001. The contrived acronym stands for Uniting and Strengthening America by Providing Appropriate Tools Required to Intercept and Obstruct Terrorism Act of 2001 (Public Law Pub.L. 107-56.)
Rules of origin	Rules of origin are used to determine the country of origin of a product for purposes of international trade. There are two common type of Rules of origin depending upon application, the preferential and non-preferential Rules of origin The exact rules vary from country to country.
Duty	Duty (from "due," that which is owing, O. Fr. deu, did, past participle of devoir; Lat. debere, debitum; cf.

Chapter 9. GATT Law and the World Trade Organization: Basic Principles

Tariff	A Tariff is a duty imposed on goods when they are moved across a political boundary. They are usually associated with protectionism, the economic policy of restraining trade between nations. For political reasons, Tariff s are usually imposed on imported goods, although they may also be imposed on exported goods.
World Trade Organization	The World Trade Organization is an important selective, mainly private, international organization designed by its founders to supervise and liberalize international trade. The organization officially commenced on 1 January 1995, under the Marrakesh Agreement, succeeding the 1947 General Agreement on Tariffs and Trade (GATT.) The World Trade Organization deals with regulation of trade between participating countries; it provides a framework for negotiating and formalising trade agreements, and a dispute resolution process aimed at enforcing participants" adherence to World Trade Organization agreements which are signed by representatives of member governments and ratified by their parliaments.
Franchising	Franchising refers to the methods of practicing and using another person"s business philosophy. The franchisor grants the independent operator the right to distribute its products, techniques, and trademarks for a percentage of gross monthly sales and a royalty fee. Various tangibles and intangibles such as national or international advertising, training, and other support services are commonly made available by the franchisor.
Trade in Service	Trade in Services refers to the sale and delivery of an intangible product, called a service, between a producer and consumer. Trade in services takes place between a producer and consumer that are, in legal terms, based in different countries, or economies, this is called International Trade in Services. International trade in services is defined by the Four Modes of Supply of the General Agreement on Trade in Services (GATS.)
Trademark	A trademark or trade mark is a distinctive sign or indicator used by an individual, business organization and to distinguish its products or services from those of other entities. A trademark is designated by the following symbols: · â„¢ (for an unregistered trademark that is, a mark used to promote or brand goods); · â„ (for an unregistered service mark, that is, a mark used to promote or brand services); and · Â® (for a registered trademark) A trademark is a type of intellectual property, and typically a name, word, phrase, logo, symbol, design, image, or a combination of these elements. There is also a range of non-conventional trademark s comprising marks which do not fall into these standard categories. The owner of a registered trademark may commence legal proceedings for trademark infringement to prevent unauthorized use of that trademark
World Bank	The World Bank is an international financial institution that provides financial and technical assistance to developing countries for development programs (e.g. bridges, roads, schools, etc.) with the stated goal of reducing poverty. The World Bank differs from the World Bank Group, in that the World Bank comprises only two institutions:

· International Bank for Reconstruction and Development (IBRD)
· International Development Association (IDA)
Whereas the latter incorporates these two in addition to three more:

· International Finance Corporation (IFC)
· Multilateral Investment Guarantee Agency (MIGA)
· International Centre for Settlement of Investment Disputes (ICSID) John Maynard Keynes (right) represented the UK at the conference, and Harry Dexter White represented the US.
The World Bank is one of two major financial institutions created as a result of the Bretton Woods Conference in 1944. The International Monetary Fund, a related but separate institution, is the second.

WTO

The WTO (WTO) is an international organization designed by its founders to supervise and liberalize international trade. The organization officially commenced on 1 January 1995, under the Marrakesh Agreement, succeeding the 1947 General Agreement on Tariffs and Trade (GATT.)
The WTO deals with regulation of trade between participating countries; it provides a framework for negotiating and formalising trade agreements, and a dispute resolution process aimed at enforcing participants" adherence to WTO agreements which are signed by representatives of member governments and ratified by their parliaments.

Precedent

In common law legal systems, a Precedent or authority is a legal case establishing a principle or rule that a court or other judicial body utilizes when deciding subsequent cases with similar issues or facts. The Precedent on an issue is the collective body of judicially announced principles that a court should consider when interpreting the law. When a Precedent establishes an important legal principle, or represents a new or changed law on a particular issue, that Precedent is often known as a landmark decision.

United States

· History of competition law
· Monopoly

· Coercive monopoly
· Natural monopoly
· Barriers to entry
· Market power
· SSNIP test
· Relevant market
· Merger control

Anti-competitive practices

· Monopolization
· Collusion

· Formation of cartels
· Price fixing
· Bid rigging
· Product bundling and tying
· Refusal to deal

· Group boycott
· Exclusive dealing
· Dividing territories
· Conscious parallelism
· Predatory pricing
· Misuse of patents and copyrights

Laws and doctrines

United States

· Sherman Antitrust Act
· Clayton Antitrust Act
· Robinson-Patman Act
· FTC Act
· Hart-Scott-Rodino Act
· Merger guidelines
· Essential facilities doctrine
· Noerr-Pennington doctrine
· Parker immunity doctrine
· Rule of reason

Europe

· UK competition law
· Irish competition law

Australia

· Trade Practices Act 1974

Enforcement authorities and organizations

Competition law history refers to attempts by governments to regulate competitive markets for goods and services, leading up to the modern competition or antitrust laws around the world today. The earliest records traces back to the efforts of Roman legislators to control price fluctuations and unfair trade practices. Through the Middle Ages in Europe, Kings and Queens repeatedly cracked down on monopolies, including those created through state legislation.

· International Competition Network
· List of competition regulators

Numerary	Numerary is a civil designation for persons who are incorporated in a fixed or permanent way to a society or group: regular member of the working staff, permanent staff distinguished from a super Numerary .
	The term Numerary and its counterpart, "super Numerary ," originated in Spanish and Latin American academy and government; it is now also used in countries all over the world, such as France, the U.S., England, Italy, etc.
	There are Numerary members of surgical organizations, of universities, of gastronomical associations, etc.
Arbitration	Arbitration, a form of alternative dispute resolution (ADR), is a legal technique for the resolution of disputes outside the courts, wherein the parties to a dispute refer it to one or more persons (the "arbitrators", "arbiters" or "arbitral tribunal"), by whose decision (the "award") they agree to be bound. It is a settlement technique in which a third party reviews the case and imposes a decision that is legally binding for both sides. Other forms of ADR include mediation (a form of settlement negotiation facilitated by a neutral third party) and non-binding resolution by experts.

84

Consumer Product Safety Commission	The United States Consumer Product Safety Commission is an independent agency of the United States government created in 1972 through the Consumer Product Safety Act to protect "against unreasonable risks of injuries associated with consumer products." As of 2006 its acting chairman is Nancy Nord, a Republican. The other commissioner is Thomas Hill Moore, a Democrat. Normally the board has three commissioners.
Three-card Monte	Three-card Monte Three-card trick, Three-Way, Three-card shuffle, Menage-a-card, Triplets, Follow the lady, Find the lady or mark, is tricked into betting a sum of money that they can find the money card, for example the queen of hearts, among three face-down playing cards. In its full form, the Three-card Monte is an example of a classic short con in which the outside man pretends to conspire with the mark to cheat the inside man, while in fact conspiring with the inside man to cheat the mark. This confidence trick has a great deal in common with the shell game; they are the same except that cards are used instead of "shells".
Franchising	Franchising refers to the methods of practicing and using another person"s business philosophy. The franchisor grants the independent operator the right to distribute its products, techniques, and trademarks for a percentage of gross monthly sales and a royalty fee. Various tangibles and intangibles such as national or international advertising, training, and other support services are commonly made available by the franchisor.
Trade in Service	Trade in Services refers to the sale and delivery of an intangible product, called a service, between a producer and consumer. Trade in services takes place between a producer and consumer that are, in legal terms, based in different countries, or economies, this is called International Trade in Services. International trade in services is defined by the Four Modes of Supply of the General Agreement on Trade in Services (GATS.)
North American Free Trade Agreement	The North American Free Trade Agreement is a trilateral trade bloc in North America created by the governments of the United States, Canada, and Mexico. The agreement creating the trade bloc came into force on January 1, 1994. It superseded the Canada-United States Free Trade Agreement between the U.S. and Canada.
Contract	Agreement is said to be reached when an offer capable of immediate acceptance is met with a "mirror image" acceptance (ie, an unqualified acceptance). The parties must have the necessary capacity to Contract and the Contract must not be either trifling, indeterminate, impossible or illegal. Contract law is based on the principle expressed in the Latin phrase pacta sunt servanda .
World Trade Organization	The World Trade Organization is an important selective, mainly private, international organization designed by its founders to supervise and liberalize international trade. The organization officially commenced on 1 January 1995, under the Marrakesh Agreement, succeeding the 1947 General Agreement on Tariffs and Trade (GATT.) The World Trade Organization deals with regulation of trade between participating countries; it provides a framework for negotiating and formalising trade agreements, and a dispute resolution process aimed at enforcing participants" adherence to World Trade Organization agreements which are signed by representatives of member governments and ratified by their parliaments.

Agreement on Trade Related Aspects of Intellectual Property Rights	The Agreement on Trade Related Aspects of Intellectual Property Rights is an international agreement administered by the World Trade Organization (WTO) that sets down minimum standards for many forms of intellectual property (IP) regulation. It was negotiated at the end of the Uruguay Round of the General Agreement on Tariffs and Trade (GATT) in 1994.
	Specifically, TRIPS contains requirements that nations" laws must meet for: copyright rights, including the rights of performers, producers of sound recordings and broadcasting organizations; geographical indications, including appellations of origin; industrial designs; integrated circuit layout-designs; patents; monopolies for the developers of new plant varieties; trademarks; trade dress; and undisclosed or confidential information.
United Nations Conference on Trade and Development	The United Nations Conference on Trade and Development was established in 1964 as a permanent intergovernmental body. It is the principal organ of the United Nations General Assembly dealing with trade, investment and development issues.
	The organization"s goals are to "maximize the trade, investment and development opportunities of developing countries and assist them in their efforts to integrate into the world economy on an equitable basis." (from official website.)
United States	

· History of competition law
· Monopoly

· Coercive monopoly
· Natural monopoly
· Barriers to entry
· Market power
· SSNIP test
· Relevant market
· Merger control

Anti-competitive practices

· Monopolization
· Collusion

· Formation of cartels
· Price fixing
· Bid rigging
· Product bundling and tying
· Refusal to deal

89

· Group boycott
· Exclusive dealing
· Dividing territories
· Conscious parallelism
· Predatory pricing
· Misuse of patents and copyrights

Laws and doctrines

United States

· Sherman Antitrust Act
· Clayton Antitrust Act
· Robinson-Patman Act
· FTC Act
· Hart-Scott-Rodino Act
· Merger guidelines
· Essential facilities doctrine
· Noerr-Pennington doctrine
· Parker immunity doctrine
· Rule of reason

Europe

· UK competition law
· Irish competition law

Australia

· Trade Practices Act 1974

Enforcement authorities and organizations

Competition law history refers to attempts by governments to regulate competitive markets for goods and services, leading up to the modern competition or antitrust laws around the world today. The earliest records traces back to the efforts of Roman legislators to control price fluctuations and unfair trade practices. Through the Middle Ages in Europe, Kings and Queens repeatedly cracked down on monopolies, including those created through state legislation.

· International Competition Network
· List of competition regulators

90

Tariff	A Tariff is a duty imposed on goods when they are moved across a political boundary. They are usually associated with protectionism, the economic policy of restraining trade between nations. For political reasons, Tariff s are usually imposed on imported goods, although they may also be imposed on exported goods.
World Trade Organization	The World Trade Organization is an important selective, mainly private, international organization designed by its founders to supervise and liberalize international trade. The organization officially commenced on 1 January 1995, under the Marrakesh Agreement, succeeding the 1947 General Agreement on Tariffs and Trade (GATT.) The World Trade Organization deals with regulation of trade between participating countries; it provides a framework for negotiating and formalising trade agreements, and a dispute resolution process aimed at enforcing participants" adherence to World Trade Organization agreements which are signed by representatives of member governments and ratified by their parliaments.
Escape clause	An Escape clause is any clause, term or condition in a contract that allows a party to that contract to avoid having to perform the contract. If an agreement was drawn up for the sale of a house, for example, the purchaser could include some kind of Escape clause in the contract, which will allow him to "escape" from the contract without being liable for breach of contract. A "Subject to a builder"s inspection to purchaser"s full satisfaction" clause is one example of an Escape clause.
United States	· History of competition law · Monopoly

      · Coercive monopoly
      · Natural monopoly
      · Barriers to entry
      · Market power
      · SSNIP test
      · Relevant market
      · Merger control

Anti-competitive practices

      · Monopolization
      · Collusion

      · Formation of cartels
      · Price fixing
      · Bid rigging
      · Product bundling and tying
      · Refusal to deal

- Group boycott
- Exclusive dealing
- Dividing territories
- Conscious parallelism
- Predatory pricing
- Misuse of patents and copyrights

Laws and doctrines

United States

- Sherman Antitrust Act
- Clayton Antitrust Act
- Robinson-Patman Act
- FTC Act
- Hart-Scott-Rodino Act
- Merger guidelines
- Essential facilities doctrine
- Noerr-Pennington doctrine
- Parker immunity doctrine
- Rule of reason

Europe

- UK competition law
- Irish competition law

Australia

- Trade Practices Act 1974

Enforcement authorities and organizations

Competition law history refers to attempts by governments to regulate competitive markets for goods and services, leading up to the modern competition or antitrust laws around the world today. The earliest records traces back to the efforts of Roman legislators to control price fluctuations and unfair trade practices. Through the Middle Ages in Europe, Kings and Queens repeatedly cracked down on monopolies, including those created through state legislation.

- International Competition Network
- List of competition regulators

WTO

The WTO (WTO) is an international organization designed by its founders to supervise and liberalize international trade. The organization officially commenced on 1 January 1995, under the Marrakesh Agreement, succeeding the 1947 General Agreement on Tariffs and Trade (GATT.)

The WTO deals with regulation of trade between participating countries; it provides a framework for negotiating and formalising trade agreements, and a dispute resolution process aimed at enforcing participants" adherence to WTO agreements which are signed by representatives of member governments and ratified by their parliaments.

95

Job interview	A Job interview is a process in which a potential employee is evaluated by an employer for prospective employment in their company, organization and was established in the late 16th century.
	A Job interview typically precedes the hiring decision, and is used to evaluate the candidate. The interview is usually preceded by the evaluation of submitted résumés from interested candidates, then selecting a small number of candidates for interviews.
United Nations Commission on International Trade Law	The United Nations Commission on International Trade Law was established by the United Nations General Assembly by its Resolution 2205 (XXI) of 17 December 1966 "to promote the progressive harmonization and unification of international trade law.
	UNCITRAL carries out its work at annual sessions held alternately in New York City and Vienna.
	When world trade began to expand dramatically in the 1960s, national governments began to realize the need for a global set of standards and rules to harmonize national and regional regulations, which until then governed international trade.
United Nations Conference on Trade and Development	The United Nations Conference on Trade and Development was established in 1964 as a permanent intergovernmental body. It is the principal organ of the United Nations General Assembly dealing with trade, investment and development issues.
	The organization"s goals are to "maximize the trade, investment and development opportunities of developing countries and assist them in their efforts to integrate into the world economy on an equitable basis." (from official website.)

Tariff

A Tariff is a duty imposed on goods when they are moved across a political boundary. They are usually associated with protectionism, the economic policy of restraining trade between nations. For political reasons, Tariff s are usually imposed on imported goods, although they may also be imposed on exported goods.

United States

· History of competition law
· Monopoly

· Coercive monopoly
· Natural monopoly
· Barriers to entry
· Market power
· SSNIP test
· Relevant market
· Merger control

Anti-competitive practices

· Monopolization
· Collusion

· Formation of cartels
· Price fixing
· Bid rigging
· Product bundling and tying
· Refusal to deal

· Group boycott
· Exclusive dealing
· Dividing territories
· Conscious parallelism
· Predatory pricing
· Misuse of patents and copyrights

Laws and doctrines

United States

· Sherman Antitrust Act
· Clayton Antitrust Act
· Robinson-Patman Act
· FTC Act
· Hart-Scott-Rodino Act
· Merger guidelines
· Essential facilities doctrine
· Noerr-Pennington doctrine
· Parker immunity doctrine
· Rule of reason

99

Europe

· UK competition law
· Irish competition law
Australia

· Trade Practices Act 1974

Enforcement authorities and organizations

Competition law history refers to attempts by governments to regulate competitive markets for goods and services, leading up to the modern competition or antitrust laws around the world today. The earliest records traces back to the efforts of Roman legislators to control price fluctuations and unfair trade practices. Through the Middle Ages in Europe, Kings and Queens repeatedly cracked down on monopolies, including those created through state legislation.

· International Competition Network
· List of competition regulators

Liquidation	In law, Liquidation refers to the process by which a company (or part of a company) is brought to an end, and the assets and property of the company redistributed. Liquidation can also be referred to as winding-up or dissolution, although dissolution technically refers to the last stage of Liquidation. The process of Liquidation also arises when customs, an authority or agency in a country responsible for collecting and safeguarding customs duties, determines the final computation or ascertainment of the duties or drawback accruing on an entry.
Competition law	Competition law, known in the United States as antitrust law, has three main elements: · prohibiting agreements or practices that restrict free trading and competition between business entities. This includes in particular the repression of cartels. · banning abusive behavior by a firm dominating a market, or anti-competitive practices that tend to lead to such a dominant position.
Reasonable care	In tort law, a duty of care is a legal obligation imposed on an individual requiring that they adhere to a standard of reasonable care while performing any acts that could foreseeably harm others. It is the first element that must be established to proceed with an action in negligence. The plaintiff must be able to articulate a duty of care imposed by law which the defendant has breached.
Statute	A statute is a formal written enactment of a legislative authority that governs a country, state, city, or county. Typically, statute s command or prohibit something, or declare policy. The word is often used to distinguish law made by legislative bodies from case law and the regulations issued by Government agencies.

Statute of limitations	A statute of limitations is a statute in a common law legal system that sets forth the maximum period of time, after certain events, that legal proceedings based on those events may be initiated. In civil law systems, similar provisions are usually part of the civil code or criminal code and are often known collectively as "periods of prescription" or "prescriptive periods."
	A common law legal system might have a statute limiting the time for prosecution of crimes called misdemeanors to two years after the offense occurred. In that statute, if a person is discovered to have committed a misdemeanor three years ago, the time has expired for the prosecution of the misdemeanor.
Duty	Duty (from "due," that which is owing, O. Fr. deu, did, past participle of devoir; Lat. debere, debitum; cf.
Chief brand officer	A Chief brand officer is a relatively new executive level position at a corporation, company, organization typically reporting directly to the CEO or board of directors. The Chief brand officer is responsible for a brand"s image, experience, and promise, and propagating it throughout all aspects of the company. The brand officer oversees marketing, advertising, design, public relations and customer service departments.
Rules of Origin	Rules of origin are used to determine the country of origin of a product for purposes of international trade. There are two common type of Rules of origin depending upon application, the preferential and non-preferential Rules of origin The exact rules vary from country to country.
Federal Trade Commission	The Federal Trade Commission is an independent agency of the United States government, established in 1914 by the Federal Trade Commission Act. Its principal mission is the promotion of "consumer protection" and the elimination and prevention of what regulators perceive to be harmfully "anti-competitive" business practices, such as coercive monopoly.
	The Federal Trade Commission Act was one of President Wilson"s major acts against trusts.
Three-card Monte	Three-card Monte Three-card trick, Three-Way, Three-card shuffle, Menage-a-card, Triplets, Follow the lady, Find the lady or mark, is tricked into betting a sum of money that they can find the money card, for example the queen of hearts, among three face-down playing cards. In its full form, the Three-card Monte is an example of a classic short con in which the outside man pretends to conspire with the mark to cheat the inside man, while in fact conspiring with the inside man to cheat the mark.
	This confidence trick has a great deal in common with the shell game; they are the same except that cards are used instead of "shells".
North American Free Trade Agreement	The North American Free Trade Agreement is a trilateral trade bloc in North America created by the governments of the United States, Canada, and Mexico. The agreement creating the trade bloc came into force on January 1, 1994. It superseded the Canada-United States Free Trade Agreement between the U.S. and Canada.

Partnership

A Partnership is a type of business entity in which partners (owners) share with each other the profits or losses of the business. Partnership s are often favored over corporations for taxation purposes, as the Partnership structure does not generally incur a tax on profits before it is distributed to the partners (i.e. there is no dividend tax levied.) However, depending on the Partnership structure and the jurisdiction in which it operates, owners of a Partnership may be exposed to greater personal liability than they would as shareholders of a corporation.

Chapter 13. North American Free Trade Law

North American Free Trade Agreement	The North American Free Trade Agreement is a trilateral trade bloc in North America created by the governments of the United States, Canada, and Mexico. The agreement creating the trade bloc came into force on January 1, 1994. It superseded the Canada-United States Free Trade Agreement between the U.S. and Canada.
Tariff	A Tariff is a duty imposed on goods when they are moved across a political boundary. They are usually associated with protectionism, the economic policy of restraining trade between nations. For political reasons, Tariff s are usually imposed on imported goods, although they may also be imposed on exported goods.
Competition law	Competition law, known in the United States as antitrust law, has three main elements:

· prohibiting agreements or practices that restrict free trading and competition between business entities. This includes in particular the repression of cartels.
· banning abusive behavior by a firm dominating a market, or anti-competitive practices that tend to lead to such a dominant position.

United States

· History of competition law
· Monopoly

· Coercive monopoly
· Natural monopoly
· Barriers to entry
· Market power
· SSNIP test
· Relevant market
· Merger control

Anti-competitive practices

· Monopolization
· Collusion

· Formation of cartels
· Price fixing
· Bid rigging
· Product bundling and tying
· Refusal to deal

· Group boycott
· Exclusive dealing
· Dividing territories
· Conscious parallelism
· Predatory pricing
· Misuse of patents and copyrights

Laws and doctrines

107

United States

· Sherman Antitrust Act
· Clayton Antitrust Act
· Robinson-Patman Act
· FTC Act
· Hart-Scott-Rodino Act
· Merger guidelines
· Essential facilities doctrine
· Noerr-Pennington doctrine
· Parker immunity doctrine
· Rule of reason

Europe

· UK competition law
· Irish competition law

Australia

· Trade Practices Act 1974

Enforcement authorities and organizations

Competition law history refers to attempts by governments to regulate competitive markets for goods and services, leading up to the modern competition or antitrust laws around the world today. The earliest records traces back to the efforts of Roman legislators to control price fluctuations and unfair trade practices. Through the Middle Ages in Europe, Kings and Queens repeatedly cracked down on monopolies, including those created through state legislation.

· International Competition Network
· List of competition regulators

Rules of origin	Rules of origin are used to determine the country of origin of a product for purposes of international trade. There are two common type of Rules of origin depending upon application, the preferential and non-preferential Rules of origin The exact rules vary from country to country.
Three-card Monte	Three-card Monte Three-card trick, Three-Way, Three-card shuffle, Menage-a-card, Triplets, Follow the lady, Find the lady or mark, is tricked into betting a sum of money that they can find the money card, for example the queen of hearts, among three face-down playing cards. In its full form, the Three-card Monte is an example of a classic short con in which the outside man pretends to conspire with the mark to cheat the inside man, while in fact conspiring with the inside man to cheat the mark. This confidence trick has a great deal in common with the shell game; they are the same except that cards are used instead of "shells".
Trade in Service	Trade in Services refers to the sale and delivery of an intangible product, called a service, between a producer and consumer. Trade in services takes place between a producer and consumer that are, in legal terms, based in different countries, or economies, this is called International Trade in Services.

International trade in services is defined by the Four Modes of Supply of the General Agreement on Trade in Services (GATS.)

Job interview

A Job interview is a process in which a potential employee is evaluated by an employer for prospective employment in their company, organization and was established in the late 16th century.

A Job interview typically precedes the hiring decision, and is used to evaluate the candidate. The interview is usually preceded by the evaluation of submitted résumés from interested candidates, then selecting a small number of candidates for interviews.

Constitution

· Apostolic Constitution (a class of Roman Catholic Church documents)
· Constitution of the Roman Republic
· Constitutional court
· Constitutionalism
· Corporate Constitution
· Judicial activism
· Judicial restraint
· Judicial review
Judicial philosophies of Constitutional interpretation (note: generally specific to United States Constitutional law)

· List of national Constitutions
· Originalism
· Strict constructionism
· Textualism
· Proposed European Union Constitution

· Treaty of Lisbon (adopts same changes, but without Constitutional name)
· United Nations Charter

United States

· History of competition law
· Monopoly

· Coercive monopoly
· Natural monopoly
· Barriers to entry
· Market power
· SSNIP test
· Relevant market
· Merger control

Anti-competitive practices

· Monopolization
· Collusion

· Formation of cartels
· Price fixing
· Bid rigging
· Product bundling and tying
· Refusal to deal

· Group boycott
· Exclusive dealing
· Dividing territories
· Conscious parallelism
· Predatory pricing
· Misuse of patents and copyrights

Laws and doctrines

United States

· Sherman Antitrust Act
· Clayton Antitrust Act
· Robinson-Patman Act
· FTC Act
· Hart-Scott-Rodino Act
· Merger guidelines
· Essential facilities doctrine
· Noerr-Pennington doctrine
· Parker immunity doctrine
· Rule of reason

Europe

· UK competition law
· Irish competition law

Australia

· Trade Practices Act 1974

Enforcement authorities and organizations

Competition law history refers to attempts by governments to regulate competitive markets for goods and services, leading up to the modern competition or antitrust laws around the world today. The earliest records traces back to the efforts of Roman legislators to control price fluctuations and unfair trade practices. Through the Middle Ages in Europe, Kings and Queens repeatedly cracked down on monopolies, including those created through state legislation.

· International Competition Network
· List of competition regulators

Separation of powers	The separation of powers is a model for the governance of democratic states. The model was first developed in ancient Greece and came into widespread use by the Roman Republic as part of the uncodified Constitution of the Roman Republic. Under this model, the state is divided into branches or estates, each with separate and independent powers and areas of responsibility.
WTO	The WTO (WTO) is an international organization designed by its founders to supervise and liberalize international trade. The organization officially commenced on 1 January 1995, under the Marrakesh Agreement, succeeding the 1947 General Agreement on Tariffs and Trade (GATT.)

The WTO deals with regulation of trade between participating countries; it provides a framework for negotiating and formalising trade agreements, and a dispute resolution process aimed at enforcing participants" adherence to WTO agreements which are signed by representatives of member governments and ratified by their parliaments.

Privacy

Privacy is the ability of an individual or group to seclude themselves or information about themselves and thereby reveal themselves selectively. The boundaries and content of what is considered private differ among cultures and individuals, but share basic common themes. Privacy is sometimes related to anonymity, the wish to remain unnoticed or unidentified in the public realm.

Business

There are many ways in which a business may be owned under the legal system of England and Wales. Different types of ownership are suitable for organisations depending on the degree of control the owners wish to have over the business. The choice of ownership methor also relates to the organisations ability to raise funds for the business activities.

ISO

The International Organization for Standardization (Organisation internationale de normalisation), widely known as ISO , is an international-standard-setting body composed of representatives from various national standards organizations. Founded on 23 February 1947, the organization promulgates worldwide proprietary industrial and commercial standards. It has its headquarters in Geneva, Switzerland.

Competition law

Competition law, known in the United States as antitrust law, has three main elements:

· prohibiting agreements or practices that restrict free trading and competition between business entities. This includes in particular the repression of cartels.
· banning abusive behavior by a firm dominating a market, or anti-competitive practices that tend to lead to such a dominant position.

USA PATRIOT Act	The USA Patriot Act, commonly known as the "Patriot Act", is a statute enacted by the United States Government that President George W. Bush signed into law on October 26, 2001. The contrived acronym stands for Uniting and Strengthening America by Providing Appropriate Tools Required to Intercept and Obstruct Terrorism Act of 2001 (Public Law Pub.L. 107-56.)
Wassenaar Arrangement	The Wassenaar Arrangement is a multilateral export control regime (MECR) with 40 participating states. It is the successor to the Cold war-era Coordinating Committee for Multilateral Export Controls (COCOM), and was established on May 12, 1996, in the Dutch town of Wassenaar, near The Hague. The Wassenaar Arrangement is considerably less strict than COCOM, focusing primarily on the transparency of national export control regimes and not granting veto power to individual members over organizational decisions.
Employment	Employment is a contract between two parties, one being the employer and the other being the employee. An employee may be defined as: "A person in the service of another under any contract of hire, express or implied, oral or written, where the employer has the power or right to control and direct the employee in the material details of how the work is to be performed." Black"s Law Dictionary page 471 (5th ed. 1979).
Labor law	Labor law (or employment law) is the body of laws, administrative rulings, and precedents which address the legal rights of, and restrictions on, working people and their organizations. As such, it mediates many aspects of the relationship between trade unions, employers and employees. In Canada, employment laws related to unionized workplaces are differentiated from those relating to particular individuals.
License	The verb License or grant License means to give permission. The noun License refers to that permission as well as to the document memorializing that permission. License may be granted by a party to another party as an element of an agreement between those parties.
Arbitration	Arbitration, a form of alternative dispute resolution (ADR), is a legal technique for the resolution of disputes outside the courts, wherein the parties to a dispute refer it to one or more persons (the "arbitrators", "arbiters" or "arbitral tribunal"), by whose decision (the "award") they agree to be bound. It is a settlement technique in which a third party reviews the case and imposes a decision that is legally binding for both sides. Other forms of ADR include mediation (a form of settlement negotiation facilitated by a neutral third party) and non-binding resolution by experts.
Arbitration award	An Arbitration award (or arbitral award) is a determination on the merits by an arbitration tribunal in an arbitration, and is analogous to a judgment in a court of law. It is referred to as an "award" even where all of the claimant"s claims fail (and thus no money needs to be paid by either party), or the award is of a non-monetary nature. Although Arbitration awards are characteristically an award of damages against a party, tribunals usually have a range of remedies that can form a part of the award.

Trading with the
Enemy Act

The Trading with the Enemy Act, sometimes abbreviated as TWEA, is a United States federal law, 12 U.S.C. §§ 95a, enacted in 1917 to restrict trade with countries hostile to the United States. The law gives the President the power to oversee or restrict any and all trade between the U.S. and her enemies in times of war.

Chief brand officer	A Chief brand officer is a relatively new executive level position at a corporation, company, organization typically reporting directly to the CEO or board of directors. The Chief brand officer is responsible for a brand"s image, experience, and promise, and propagating it throughout all aspects of the company. The brand officer oversees marketing, advertising, design, public relations and customer service departments.
Independent contractor	An Independent contractor is a natural person, business, or corporation which provides goods or services to another entity under terms specified in a contract or within a verbal agreement. Unlike an employee, an Independent contractor does not work regularly for an employer but works as and when required, during which time she or he may be subject to the Law of Agency. Independent contractors are usually paid on a freelance basis.
Contract	Agreement is said to be reached when an offer capable of immediate acceptance is met with a "mirror image" acceptance (ie, an unqualified acceptance). The parties must have the necessary capacity to Contract and the Contract must not be either trifling, indeterminate, impossible or illegal. Contract law is based on the principle expressed in the Latin phrase pacta sunt servanda .
Labor law	Labor law (or employment law) is the body of laws, administrative rulings, and precedents which address the legal rights of, and restrictions on, working people and their organizations. As such, it mediates many aspects of the relationship between trade unions, employers and employees. In Canada, employment laws related to unionized workplaces are differentiated from those relating to particular individuals.
Product liability	Product liability is the area of law in which manufacturers, distributors, suppliers, retailers, and others who make products available to the public are held responsible for the injuries those products cause. In the United States, the claims most commonly associated with Product liability are negligence, strict liability, breach of warranty, and various consumer protection claims. The majority of Product liability laws are determined at the state level and vary widely from state to state.
Employment	Employment is a contract between two parties, one being the employer and the other being the employee. An employee may be defined as: "A person in the service of another under any contract of hire, express or implied, oral or written, where the employer has the power or right to control and direct the employee in the material details of how the work is to be performed." Black"s Law Dictionary page 471 (5th ed. 1979).
Bribery	Bribery, a form of pecuniary corruption, is an act implying money or gift given that alters the behaviour of the recipient. Bribery constitutes a crime and is defined by Black"s Law Dictionary as the offering, giving, receiving, or soliciting of any item of value to influence the actions of an official or other person in discharge of a public or legal duty. The bribe is the gift bestowed to influence the recipient"s conduct.
Business	There are many ways in which a business may be owned under the legal system of England and Wales.

Different types of ownership are suitable for organisations depending on the degree of control the owners wish to have over the business. The choice of ownership methor also relates to the organisations ability to raise funds for the business activities.

101

124

Agreement on Trade Related Aspects of Intellectual Property Rights	The Agreement on Trade Related Aspects of Intellectual Property Rights is an international agreement administered by the World Trade Organization (WTO) that sets down minimum standards for many forms of intellectual property (IP) regulation. It was negotiated at the end of the Uruguay Round of the General Agreement on Tariffs and Trade (GATT) in 1994. Specifically, TRIPS contains requirements that nations" laws must meet for: copyright rights, including the rights of performers, producers of sound recordings and broadcasting organizations; geographical indications, including appellations of origin; industrial designs; integrated circuit layout-designs; patents; monopolies for the developers of new plant varieties; trademarks; trade dress; and undisclosed or confidential information.
Patent	A patent is a set of exclusive rights granted by a state to an inventor or his assignee for a limited period of time in exchange for a disclosure of an invention. The procedure for granting patent s, the requirements placed on the patent ee and the extent of the exclusive rights vary widely between countries according to national laws and international agreements. Typically, however, a patent application must include one or more claims defining the invention which must be new, inventive, and useful or industrially applicable.
Patent Cooperation Treaty	The Patent Cooperation Treaty is an international patent law treaty, concluded in 1970. It provides a unified procedure for filing patent applications to protect inventions in each of its Contracting States A patent application filed under the Patent Cooperation Treaty is called an international application or Patent Cooperation Treaty application.
World Intellectual Property Organization	The World Intellectual Property Organization is one of the 16 specialized agencies of the United Nations. World Intellectual Property Organization was created in 1967 "to encourage creative activity, to promote the protection of intellectual property throughout the world". World Intellectual Property Organization currently has 184 member states, administers 24 international treaties, and is headquartered in Geneva, Switzerland.
Competition law	Competition law, known in the United States as antitrust law, has three main elements: · prohibiting agreements or practices that restrict free trading and competition between business entities. This includes in particular the repression of cartels. · banning abusive behavior by a firm dominating a market, or anti-competitive practices that tend to lead to such a dominant position.
Trademark	A trademark or trade mark is a distinctive sign or indicator used by an individual, business organization and to distinguish its products or services from those of other entities. A trademark is designated by the following symbols: · â„¢ (for an unregistered trademark that is, a mark used to promote or brand goods); · â„ (for an unregistered service mark, that is, a mark used to promote or brand services); and · Â® (for a registered trademark) A trademark is a type of intellectual property, and typically a name, word, phrase, logo, symbol, design, image, or a combination of these elements. There is also a range of non-conventional trademark s comprising marks which do not fall into these standard categories.

The owner of a registered trademark may commence legal proceedings for trademark infringement to prevent unauthorized use of that trademark

Uniform Domain-Name Dispute-Resolution Policy	The Uniform Domain-Name Dispute-Resolution Policy is a process established by the Internet Corporation for Assigned Names and Numbers (ICANN) for the resolution of disputes regarding the registration of internet domain names. The UDRP currently applies to all .biz, .com, .info, .name, .net, and .org top-level domains, and some country code top-level domains.
	When a registrant chooses a domain name, the registrant must "represent and warrant," among other things, that registering the name "will not infringe upon or otherwise violate the rights of any third party," and agree to participate in an arbitration-like proceeding should any third party assert such a claim.
Paris Convention for the Protection of Industrial Property	The Paris Convention for the Protection of Industrial Property, signed in Paris, France, on March 20, 1883, was one of the first intellectual property treaties. As a result of this treaty, intellectual property systems, including patents, of any contracting state are accessible to the nationals of other states party to the Convention.
	The "Convention priority right", also called "Paris Convention priority right" or "Union priority right", was also established by this treaty.
Regulatory	Regulation refers to "controlling human or societal behaviour by rules or restrictions." Regulation can take many forms: legal restrictions promulgated by a government authority, self-regulation, social regulation (e.g. norms), co-regulation and market regulation. One can consider regulation as actions of conduct imposing sanctions (such as a fine.) This action of administrative law, or implementing regulatory law, may be contrasted with statutory or case law.
Franchising	Franchising refers to the methods of practicing and using another person"s business philosophy. The franchisor grants the independent operator the right to distribute its products, techniques, and trademarks for a percentage of gross monthly sales and a royalty fee. Various tangibles and intangibles such as national or international advertising, training, and other support services are commonly made available by the franchisor.
Franchise tax	Franchise tax is a tax charged by some US states to corporations formed in those states based on the number of shares they issue or, in some cases, the amount of their assets. The purpose of the tax is to raise revenue for the state. The State of Delaware has a significant Franchise tax, while other states, such as Nevada, have none at all or a smaller one.

Corporate law	Corporate law (also "company" or "corporations" law) is the law of the most dominant kind of business enterprise in the modern world. Corporate law is the study of how shareholders, directors, employees, creditors, and other stakeholders such as consumers, the community and the environment interact with one another under the internal rules of the firm. Corporate law is a part of a broader companies law (or law of business associations).
Insider trading	Insider trading is the trading of a corporation"s stock or other securities (e.g. bonds or stock options) by individuals with potential access to non-public information about the company. In most countries, trading by corporate insiders such as officers, key employees, directors, and large shareholders may be legal, if this trading is done in a way that does not take advantage of non-public information. However, the term is frequently used to refer to a practice in which an insider or a related party trades based on material non-public information obtained during the performance of the insider"s duties at the corporation, or otherwise in breach of a fiduciary duty or other relationship of trust and confidence or where the non-public information was misappropriated from the company.
Joint venture	A Joint venture is an entity formed between two or more parties to undertake economic activity together. The parties agree to create a new entity by both contributing equity, and they then share in the revenues, expenses, and control of the enterprise. The venture can be for one specific project only, or a continuing business relationship such as the Fuji Xerox Joint venture.
Subsidiary	A subsidiary, in business matters, is an entity that is controlled by a bigger and more powerful entity. The controlled entity is called a company, corporation, or limited liability company and in some cases can be a government or state-owned enterprise, and the controlling entity is called its parent (or the parent company.) The reason for this distinction is that a lone company cannot be a subsidiary of any organization; only an entity representing a legal fiction as a separate entity can be a subsidiary.
Value added	Value added refers to the difference between the cost of materials purchased by a company plus the cost of the labor to assemble a product and the price at which the company sells the product. An example is the price of gasoline at the pump over the price of the oil in it. In national accounts used in macroeconomics, it refers to the contribution of the factors of production, i.e., land, labor, and capital goods, to raising the value of a product and corresponds to the incomes received by the owners of these factors.
Obligation	An obligation is a requirement to take some course of action, whether legal or moral. There are also obligation s in other normative contexts, such as obligation s of etiquette, social obligation s, and possibly in terms of politics, where obligation s are requirements which must be fulfilled. These are generally legal obligation s, which can incur a penalty for unfulfilment, although certain people are obliged to carry out certain actions for other reasons as well, whether as a tradition or for social reasons.
Structuring	Structuring, also known as smurfing in banking industry jargon, is the issue of transactions structured to avoid certain record keeping and reporting requirements mandated by law, such as the United States"s Bank Secrecy Act (BSA) and/or 26 USC 6050I (Form 8300.)

Structuring includes the act of parceling large financial transactions into smaller transactions to avoid scrutiny by regulators or law enforcement. Structuring often appears in federal indictments related to money laundering, fraud, and other financial crimes.

Tariff

A Tariff is a duty imposed on goods when they are moved across a political boundary. They are usually associated with protectionism, the economic policy of restraining trade between nations. For political reasons, Tariff s are usually imposed on imported goods, although they may also be imposed on exported goods.

United States

· History of competition law
· Monopoly

· Coercive monopoly
· Natural monopoly
· Barriers to entry
· Market power
· SSNIP test
· Relevant market
· Merger control

Anti-competitive practices

· Monopolization
· Collusion

· Formation of cartels
· Price fixing
· Bid rigging
· Product bundling and tying
· Refusal to deal

· Group boycott
· Exclusive dealing
· Dividing territories
· Conscious parallelism
· Predatory pricing
· Misuse of patents and copyrights

Laws and doctrines

United States

· Sherman Antitrust Act
· Clayton Antitrust Act
· Robinson-Patman Act
· FTC Act
· Hart-Scott-Rodino Act
· Merger guidelines
· Essential facilities doctrine
· Noerr-Pennington doctrine
· Parker immunity doctrine
· Rule of reason

135

Europe

· UK competition law
· Irish competition law
Australia

· Trade Practices Act 1974

Enforcement authorities and organizations

Competition law history refers to attempts by governments to regulate competitive markets for goods and services, leading up to the modern competition or antitrust laws around the world today. The earliest records traces back to the efforts of Roman legislators to control price fluctuations and unfair trade practices. Through the Middle Ages in Europe, Kings and Queens repeatedly cracked down on monopolies, including those created through state legislation.

· International Competition Network
· List of competition regulators

Overseas Private Investment Corporation	The Overseas Private Investment Corporation is an agency of the United States Government established in 1971 that helps U.S. businesses invest overseas and promotes economic development in new and emerging markets. Overseas Private Investment Corporation"s mission is to "foster economic development in new and emerging markets, support U.S. foreign policy and create U.S. jobs by helping U.S. businesses to invest overseas." The agency provides political risk insurance against the risks of inconvertibility, political violence, or expropriation. Overseas Private Investment Corporation also provides financing through direct loans and loan guarantees.
Chief brand officer	A Chief brand officer is a relatively new executive level position at a corporation, company, organization typically reporting directly to the CEO or board of directors. The Chief brand officer is responsible for a brand"s image, experience, and promise, and propagating it throughout all aspects of the company. The brand officer oversees marketing, advertising, design, public relations and customer service departments.
Guarantee	The act of becoming a surety is also called a Guarantee. Traditionally a Guarantee was distinguished from a surety in that the surety"s liability was joint and primary with the principal, whereas the guaranty"s liability was ancillary and derivative, but many jurisdictions have abolished this distinction
Arbitration	Arbitration, a form of alternative dispute resolution (ADR), is a legal technique for the resolution of disputes outside the courts, wherein the parties to a dispute refer it to one or more persons (the "arbitrators", "arbiters" or "arbitral tribunal"), by whose decision (the "award") they agree to be bound. It is a settlement technique in which a third party reviews the case and imposes a decision that is legally binding for both sides. Other forms of ADR include mediation (a form of settlement negotiation facilitated by a neutral third party) and non-binding resolution by experts.

Contract	Agreement is said to be reached when an offer capable of immediate acceptance is met with a "mirror image" acceptance (ie, an unqualified acceptance). The parties must have the necessary capacity to Contract and the Contract must not be either trifling, indeterminate, impossible or illegal. Contract law is based on the principle expressed in the Latin phrase pacta sunt servanda .
Breach of contract	Breach of contract is a legal concept in which a binding agreement or bargained-for exchange is not honored by one or more of the parties to the contract by non-performance or interference with the other party"s performance.
	A minor breach, a partial breach or an immaterial breach, occurs when the non-breaching party is unentitled to an order for performance of its obligations, but only to collect the actual amount of their damages. For example, suppose a homeowner hires a contractor to install new plumbing and insists that the pipes, which will ultimately be sealed behind the walls, be red.
Management contract	A Management contract is an arrangement under which operational control of an enterprise is vested by contract in a separate enterprise which performs the necessary managerial functions in return for a fee. Management contracts involve not just selling a method of doing things (as with franchising or licensing) but involves actually doing them. A Management contract can involve a wide range of functions, such as technical operation of a production facility, management of personnel, accounting, marketing services and training.
Employment	Employment is a contract between two parties, one being the employer and the other being the employee. An employee may be defined as: "A person in the service of another under any contract of hire, express or implied, oral or written, where the employer has the power or right to control and direct the employee in the material details of how the work is to be performed." Black"s Law Dictionary page 471 (5th ed. 1979).
Employment discrimination	Employment discrimination (or workplace discrimination) is discrimination in hiring, promotion, job assignment, termination, and compensation. It includes various types of harassment.
	Many jurisdictions prohibit some types of Employment discrimination, often by forbidding discrimination based on certain traits ("protected categories").
Labor law	Labor law (or employment law) is the body of laws, administrative rulings, and precedents which address the legal rights of, and restrictions on, working people and their organizations. As such, it mediates many aspects of the relationship between trade unions, employers and employees. In Canada, employment laws related to unionized workplaces are differentiated from those relating to particular individuals.
Competition law	Competition law, known in the United States as antitrust law, has three main elements:
	· prohibiting agreements or practices that restrict free trading and competition between business entities. This includes in particular the repression of cartels.
	· banning abusive behavior by a firm dominating a market, or anti-competitive practices that tend to lead to such a dominant position.

Consideration

Consideration is the legal concept of value in connection with contracts. It is anything of value in the common sense, promised to another when making a contract. It can take the form of money, physical objects, services, promised actions, or even abstinence from a future action.

Joint venture

A Joint venture is an entity formed between two or more parties to undertake economic activity together. The parties agree to create a new entity by both contributing equity, and they then share in the revenues, expenses, and control of the enterprise. The venture can be for one specific project only, or a continuing business relationship such as the Fuji Xerox Joint venture.

Chapter 20. Labor and Employment Discrimination Law

Labor law	Labor law (or employment law) is the body of laws, administrative rulings, and precedents which address the legal rights of, and restrictions on, working people and their organizations. As such, it mediates many aspects of the relationship between trade unions, employers and employees. In Canada, employment laws related to unionized workplaces are differentiated from those relating to particular individuals.
World Intellectual Property Organization	The World Intellectual Property Organization is one of the 16 specialized agencies of the United Nations. World Intellectual Property Organization was created in 1967 "to encourage creative activity, to promote the protection of intellectual property throughout the world". World Intellectual Property Organization currently has 184 member states, administers 24 international treaties, and is headquartered in Geneva, Switzerland.
Employment	Employment is a contract between two parties, one being the employer and the other being the employee. An employee may be defined as: "A person in the service of another under any contract of hire, express or implied, oral or written, where the employer has the power or right to control and direct the employee in the material details of how the work is to be performed." Black"s Law Dictionary page 471 (5th ed. 1979).
Participation	Participation, in addition to its dictionary definition, has specific meanings in certain areas. · Participation, the process of involving young people in projects, policy reviews or ideas to encourage decision-making and empowerment, ownership of opinion and influence in youth services and issues that affect them and promote inclusion (particularly used amongst marginalized groups I.e. homeless, BME communities or Ex-offenders) · Participation (decision making), a notion in theory of management, economics and politics · Participation (VR), a notion from virtual reality · Participation (ownership), sharing something in common with others · Participation (Finance), getting some benefit from the performance of a certain underlying asset · Participation constraint (ER modelling), a special case of a multiplicity constraint · e-Participation, refers to Participation in e-government, and is related to the involvement of the citizen in the democratic process. Participant redirects here. · Participant Productions .
Constitution	· Apostolic Constitution (a class of Roman Catholic Church documents) · Constitution of the Roman Republic · Constitutional court · Constitutionalism · Corporate Constitution · Judicial activism · Judicial restraint · Judicial review Judicial philosophies of Constitutional interpretation (note: generally specific to United States Constitutional law)

143

· List of national Constitutions
· Originalism
· Strict constructionism
· Textualism
· Proposed European Union Constitution

· Treaty of Lisbon (adopts same changes, but without Constitutional name)
· United Nations Charter

Employment discrimination	Employment discrimination (or workplace discrimination) is discrimination in hiring, promotion, job assignment, termination, and compensation. It includes various types of harassment. Many jurisdictions prohibit some types of Employment discrimination, often by forbidding discrimination based on certain traits ("protected categories").
Vorstand	In German corporate governance, a Vorstand is the management board of a corporation. It is controlled by the Aufsichtsrat or Supervisory Board. German law confers power on the Vorstand as an organ.
United States	

· History of competition law
· Monopoly

· Coercive monopoly
· Natural monopoly
· Barriers to entry
· Market power
· SSNIP test
· Relevant market
· Merger control

Anti-competitive practices

· Monopolization
· Collusion

· Formation of cartels
· Price fixing
· Bid rigging
· Product bundling and tying
· Refusal to deal

· Group boycott
· Exclusive dealing
· Dividing territories
· Conscious parallelism
· Predatory pricing
· Misuse of patents and copyrights

Laws and doctrines

United States

· Sherman Antitrust Act
· Clayton Antitrust Act
· Robinson-Patman Act
· FTC Act
· Hart-Scott-Rodino Act
· Merger guidelines
· Essential facilities doctrine
· Noerr-Pennington doctrine
· Parker immunity doctrine
· Rule of reason

Europe

· UK competition law
· Irish competition law

Australia

· Trade Practices Act 1974

Enforcement authorities and organizations

Competition law history refers to attempts by governments to regulate competitive markets for goods and services, leading up to the modern competition or antitrust laws around the world today. The earliest records traces back to the efforts of Roman legislators to control price fluctuations and unfair trade practices. Through the Middle Ages in Europe, Kings and Queens repeatedly cracked down on monopolies, including those created through state legislation.

· International Competition Network
· List of competition regulators

Age Discrimination in Employment Act	The Age Discrimination in Employment Act of 1967, Pub. L. No. 90-202, 81 Stat. 602 (Dec.
Tariff	A Tariff is a duty imposed on goods when they are moved across a political boundary. They are usually associated with protectionism, the economic policy of restraining trade between nations. For political reasons, Tariff s are usually imposed on imported goods, although they may also be imposed on exported goods.

Trade in Service	Trade in Services refers to the sale and delivery of an intangible product, called a service, between a producer and consumer. Trade in services takes place between a producer and consumer that are, in legal terms, based in different countries, or economies, this is called International Trade in Services. International trade in services is defined by the Four Modes of Supply of the General Agreement on Trade in Services (GATS.)
Arbitration	Arbitration, a form of alternative dispute resolution (ADR), is a legal technique for the resolution of disputes outside the courts, wherein the parties to a dispute refer it to one or more persons (the "arbitrators", "arbiters" or "arbitral tribunal"), by whose decision (the "award") they agree to be bound. It is a settlement technique in which a third party reviews the case and imposes a decision that is legally binding for both sides. Other forms of ADR include mediation (a form of settlement negotiation facilitated by a neutral third party) and non-binding resolution by experts.
Child labour	Child labour refers to the employment of children at regular and sustained labour. This practice is considered exploitative by many international organizations and is illegal in many countries. Child labour was utilized to varying extents through most of history, but entered public dispute with the advent of universal schooling, with changes in working conditions during the industrial revolution, and with the emergence of the concepts of workers" and children"s rights.
Command Center	A Command center (often called a war room) is any place that is used to provide centralised command for some purpose. While frequently considered to be a military facility, these can be used in many other cases by governments or businesses. The term "war room" is also often used in politics to refer to teams of communications people who monitor and listen to the media and the public, respond to inquiries, and synthesize opinions to determine the best course of action.
Sourcing	In business, the term word Sourcing refers to a number of procurement practices, aimed at finding, evaluating and engaging suppliers of goods and services:

· Global Sourcing a procurement strategy aimed at exploiting global efficiencies in production
· Strategic Sourcing a component of supply chain management, for improving and re-evaluating purchasing activities
● · Co Sourcing a type of auditing service
· Low-cost country Sourcing a procurement strategy for acquiring materials from countries with lower labour and production costs in order to cut operating expenses
· Corporate Sourcing a supply chain, purchasing/procurement, and inventory function
· Second-tier Sourcing a practice of rewarding suppliers for attempting to achieve minority-owned business spending goals of their customer
· Net Sourcing , a practice of utilizing an established group of businesses, individuals, or hardware ' software applications to streamline or initiate procurement practices by tapping in to and working through a third party provider
· Inverted Sourcing a price volatility reduction strategy usually conducted by procurement or supply-chain person by which the value of an organization"s waste-stream is maximized by actively seeking out the highest price possible from a range of potential buyers exploiting price trends and other market factors
· Multi Sourcing , a strategy that treats a given function, such as IT, as a portfolio of activities, some of which should be outsourced and others of which should be performed by internal staff.
· Crowd Sourcing , using an undefined, generally large group of people or community in the form of an open call to perform a task
In journalism, it can also refer to:

· Journalism Sourcing the practice of identifying a person or publication that gives information
· Single Sourcing the reuse of content in publishing
In computing, it can refer to:

· Open Sourcing the act of releasing previously proprietary software under an open source/free software license
· Power Sourcing equipment, network devices that will provide power in a Power over Ethernet (PoE) setup .

Regulatory	Regulation refers to "controlling human or societal behaviour by rules or restrictions." Regulation can take many forms: legal restrictions promulgated by a government authority, self-regulation, social regulation (e.g. norms), co-regulation and market regulation. One can consider regulation as actions of conduct imposing sanctions (such as a fine.) This action of administrative law, or implementing regulatory law, may be contrasted with statutory or case law.
Competition law	Competition law, known in the United States as antitrust law, has three main elements: · prohibiting agreements or practices that restrict free trading and competition between business entities. This includes in particular the repression of cartels. · banning abusive behavior by a firm dominating a market, or anti-competitive practices that tend to lead to such a dominant position.
Arbitration	Arbitration, a form of alternative dispute resolution (ADR), is a legal technique for the resolution of disputes outside the courts, wherein the parties to a dispute refer it to one or more persons (the "arbitrators", "arbiters" or "arbitral tribunal"), by whose decision (the "award") they agree to be bound. It is a settlement technique in which a third party reviews the case and imposes a decision that is legally binding for both sides. Other forms of ADR include mediation (a form of settlement negotiation facilitated by a neutral third party) and non-binding resolution by experts.
World Trade Organization	The World Trade Organization is an important selective, mainly private, international organization designed by its founders to supervise and liberalize international trade. The organization officially commenced on 1 January 1995, under the Marrakesh Agreement, succeeding the 1947 General Agreement on Tariffs and Trade (GATT.) The World Trade Organization deals with regulation of trade between participating countries; it provides a framework for negotiating and formalising trade agreements, and a dispute resolution process aimed at enforcing participants" adherence to World Trade Organization agreements which are signed by representatives of member governments and ratified by their parliaments.
Chief brand officer	A Chief brand officer is a relatively new executive level position at a corporation, company, organization typically reporting directly to the CEO or board of directors. The Chief brand officer is responsible for a brand"s image, experience, and promise, and propagating it throughout all aspects of the company. The brand officer oversees marketing, advertising, design, public relations and customer service departments.
Resource Conservation and Recovery Act	The Resource Conservation and Recovery Act, enacted in 1976, is the principal Federal law in the United States governing the disposal of solid waste and hazardous waste. Congress enacted RCRA to address the increasing problems the nation faced from its growing volume of municipal and industrial waste. RCRA, which amended the Solid Waste Disposal Act of 1965, set national goals for: · Protecting human health and the environment from the potential hazards of waste disposal. · Conserving energy and natural resources. · Reducing the amount of waste generated. · Ensuring that wastes are managed in an environmentally-sound manner.

EPA waste management regulations are codified at 40 C.F.R. pts. 239-282.

Toxic Substances Control Act	The Toxic Substances Control Act is a United States law, passed by the United States Congress in 1976, that regulates the introduction of new or already existing chemicals. It grandfathered most existing chemicals, in contrast to the Registration, Evaluation and Authorization of Chemicals (REACH) legislation of the European Union. However, as explained below, the Toxic Substances Control Act specifically regulates polychlorinated biphenyl (PCB) products.
Pollution	Pollution is the introduction of contaminants into an environment that causes instability, disorder, harm or discomfort to the ecosystem i.e. physical systems or living organisms . Pollution can take the form of chemical substances, or energy, such as noise, heat, or light energy. Pollutants, the elements of Pollution, can be foreign substances or energies, or naturally occurring; when naturally occurring, they are considered contaminants when they exceed natural levels.
World Bank	The World Bank is an international financial institution that provides financial and technical assistance to developing countries for development programs (e.g. bridges, roads, schools, etc.) with the stated goal of reducing poverty. The World Bank differs from the World Bank Group, in that the World Bank comprises only two institutions: · International Bank for Reconstruction and Development (IBRD) · International Development Association (IDA) Whereas the latter incorporates these two in addition to three more: · International Finance Corporation (IFC) · Multilateral Investment Guarantee Agency (MIGA) · International Centre for Settlement of Investment Disputes (ICSID) John Maynard Keynes (right) represented the UK at the conference, and Harry Dexter White represented the US. The World Bank is one of two major financial institutions created as a result of the Bretton Woods Conference in 1944. The International Monetary Fund, a related but separate institution, is the second.
Trading with the Enemy Act	The Trading with the Enemy Act, sometimes abbreviated as TWEA, is a United States federal law, 12 U.S.C. § 95a, enacted in 1917 to restrict trade with countries hostile to the United States. The law gives the President the power to oversee or restrict any and all trade between the U.S. and her enemies in times of war.
Uniform Commercial Code	The Uniform Commercial Code is one of a number of uniform acts that have been promulgated in conjunction with efforts to harmonize the law of sales and other commercial transactions in all 50 states within the United States of America. This objective is deemed important because of the prevalence today of commercial transactions that extend beyond one state (for example, where the goods are manufactured in state A, warehoused in state B, sold from state C and delivered in state D.) The Uniform Commercial Code deals primarily with transactions involving personal property (movable property), not real property (immovable property.)

154

Competition law	Competition law, known in the United States as antitrust law, has three main elements: · prohibiting agreements or practices that restrict free trading and competition between business entities. This includes in particular the repression of cartels. · banning abusive behavior by a firm dominating a market, or anti-competitive practices that tend to lead to such a dominant position.
Sherman Antitrust Act	The Sherman Antitrust Act was the first United States Federal statute to limit cartels and monopolies. It falls under antitrust law.
Regulatory	Regulation refers to "controlling human or societal behaviour by rules or restrictions." Regulation can take many forms: legal restrictions promulgated by a government authority, self-regulation, social regulation (e.g. norms), co-regulation and market regulation. One can consider regulation as actions of conduct imposing sanctions (such as a fine.) This action of administrative law, or implementing regulatory law, may be contrasted with statutory or case law.
Franchising	Franchising refers to the methods of practicing and using another person"s business philosophy. The franchisor grants the independent operator the right to distribute its products, techniques, and trademarks for a percentage of gross monthly sales and a royalty fee. Various tangibles and intangibles such as national or international advertising, training, and other support services are commonly made available by the franchisor.
Damages	Damages for breach of contract is a common law remedy, available as of right. It is designed to compensate the victim for their actual loss as a result of the wrongdoer"s breach rather than to punish the wrongdoer. If no loss has been occasioned by the plaintiff, only nominal Damages will be awarded.
Rule of reason	The Rule of reason is a doctrine developed by the United States Supreme Court in its interpretation of the Sherman Antitrust Act. The rule, stated and applied in the case of Standard Oil Co. of New Jersey v. United States, 221 U.S. 1 (1911), is that only combinations and contracts unreasonably restraining trade are subject to actions under the anti-trust laws and that size and possession of monopoly power are not illegal.
Per se	Per se: · A Latin phrase used in English arguments for "by itself" or "by themselves" It also is used in law: · Illegal per se, the legal usage of "per se" in criminal and anti-trust law · Negligence per se, legal use in tort law Other uses: · per se (restaurant), a New York City restaurant run by Thomas Keller

"Gun ownership in Japan is not, per se, illegal; however, the restrictions are such that one could easily arrive at that conclusion."

"Data trustworthiness should be attributed primarily to data per se, rather than being merely a reï¬‚ection of the trust attributed to data-reporting entities."

Employment	Employment is a contract between two parties, one being the employer and the other being the employee. An employee may be defined as: "A person in the service of another under any contract of hire, express or implied, oral or written, where the employer has the power or right to control and direct the employee in the material details of how the work is to be performed." Black"s Law Dictionary page 471 (5th ed. 1979).
Contract	Agreement is said to be reached when an offer capable of immediate acceptance is met with a "mirror image" acceptance (ie, an unqualified acceptance). The parties must have the necessary capacity to Contract and the Contract must not be either trifling, indeterminate, impossible or illegal. Contract law is based on the principle expressed in the Latin phrase pacta sunt servanda .
Sale of Goods	The sale of goods Act 1979 (c.54) is an Act of the Parliament of the United Kingdom which regulates contracts in which goods are sold and bought. The Act consolidates the sale of goods Act 1893 and subsequent legislation, which in turn consolidated the previous common law. The sale of goods Act performs several functions.
Tariff	A Tariff is a duty imposed on goods when they are moved across a political boundary. They are usually associated with protectionism, the economic policy of restraining trade between nations. For political reasons, Tariff s are usually imposed on imported goods, although they may also be imposed on exported goods.
Agreement on Trade Related Aspects of Intellectual Property Rights	The Agreement on Trade Related Aspects of Intellectual Property Rights is an international agreement administered by the World Trade Organization (WTO) that sets down minimum standards for many forms of intellectual property (IP) regulation. It was negotiated at the end of the Uruguay Round of the General Agreement on Tariffs and Trade (GATT) in 1994. Specifically, TRIPS contains requirements that nations" laws must meet for: copyright rights, including the rights of performers, producers of sound recordings and broadcasting organizations; geographical indications, including appellations of origin; industrial designs; integrated circuit layout-designs; patents; monopolies for the developers of new plant varieties; trademarks; trade dress; and undisclosed or confidential information.
North American Free Trade Agreement	The North American Free Trade Agreement is a trilateral trade bloc in North America created by the governments of the United States, Canada, and Mexico. The agreement creating the trade bloc came into force on January 1, 1994. It superseded the Canada-United States Free Trade Agreement between the U.S. and Canada.

158

CPSIA information can be obtained at www.ICGtesting.com
Printed in the USA
BVOW06s1435070414

349965BV00008B/491/P